THE
OLIVE OIL
─ COOKBOOK ─

THE
OLIVE OIL
— COOKBOOK —

LOUISE PICKFORD

SMITHMARK

This edition published in 1994 by
SMITHMARK Publishers Inc.,
16 East 32nd Street,
New York, NY 10016.

Copyright © Salamander Books Limited 1994

1 3 5 7 9 8 6 4 2

SMITHMARK books are available for bulk purchase for sales promotion
and premium use. For details write or call the manager of special sales,
SMITHMARK Publishers Inc.,
16 East 32nd Street,
New York, NY 10016;
(212) 532-6600.

ISBN 0-8317-6257-8

CREDITS
COMMISSIONING EDITOR: *Will Steeds*
EDITOR: *Miranda Spicer*
DESIGN: *The Design Revolution, Brighton, England*
PHOTOGRAPHER: *Simon Butcher*
HOME ECONOMIST: *Wendy Dines*
STYLIST: *Hilary Guy*
COLOR SEPARATION: *P & W Graphics Pte Ltd*

The publishers wish to thank Cephas Picture Library for supplying
the photographs on pages 8 (Mick Rock) and 10 (Pierre Hussenot).

Printed in Singapore

ACKNOWLEDGMENTS
I would like to thank the following people: Will Steeds and Lisa Dyer for giving me the opportunity to write this book;
Anne McDowall for her continued support, faith and encouragement; Charles Carey for his time;
Carol Tennant who helped in the testing of the recipes; and Miranda Spicer.

ABOUT THE INGREDIENTS
All herbs are fresh unless stated. Dried herbs can be substituted; 1 tablespoon chopped fresh herbs = 1 teaspoon dried.
Nuts should be toasted in a pre-heated oven at 400°F. Toast whole nuts for 10-12 minutes, chopped nuts for 8-10 minutes, ground nuts for 5 minutes.
Large eggs are used unless otherwise stated.
Salt and pepper – freshly ground black pepper and sea salt are recommended.
As seasoning is a matter of personal taste, salt and pepper are not necessarily listed in the ingredients.
Use the best quality fresh produce.

Contents

AUTHOR'S INTRODUCTION *6*

INTRODUCTION *8*

INFUSIONS, SAUCES, PASTES AND PRESERVES *14*

SOUPS AND STARTERS *26*

SEAFOOD DISHES *42*

MEAT AND POULTRY DISHES *50*

VEGETABLE DISHES *60*

SALADS *68*

PASTA AND RICE *76*

PIZZAS, BREADS, CAKES AND COOKIES *84*

INDEX *96*

Author's Introduction

During the past few years, olive oil has enjoyed a rapid increase in popularity. Food lovers worldwide have had a long-standing respect for this oil, as have the people of those countries where it is produced, yet only recently have we witnessed a growing demand for olive oil outside the oil-producing nations. This expansion is due, in part, to the versatility of olive oil as a cooking medium, but a more likely reason is recent information on the health benefits of olive oil as a source of fat in the diet. Recent medical research has indicated that olive oil may lower the level of cholesterol in the body and therefore help prevent coronary heart diseases that other fats may cause.

My passion for food stems from a childhood surrounded by fresh produce, and I inherited my love of cooking from my mother. She never used olive oil as a cooking ingredient while I was growing up and I am not even sure if any of us had heard of it, let alone tasted it. Today I cannot imagine working as a cook without it and "liquid gold" is firmly established as an essential staple in my pantry.

I fell in love with the fresh flavors of Mediterranean cooking many years ago and I soon found myself using these influences in my own cooking. Olive oil is an integral ingredient in Mediterranean dishes and often forms the basis of a recipe. The first chapter expresses this particularly well. It includes a selection of herbs, spices and aromatics steeped in olive oil, to give the oil extra flavor. Although it is probably no surprise to see olive oil listed among savory ingredients, you may not have used it in the baking of sweet things. The oil gives cakes and cookies a light texture.

The hardest part of putting this book together was deciding on which recipes to omit–the list was almost endless. I have endeavored to be as comprehensive as possible in offering an exciting and inspiring collection. Apart from Mediterranean dishes, there are also recipes with their origins in the Middle East and North and South America, which tend to be spicy.

Before cooking from this book, I recommend you read the introduction, particularly "Cooking With Olive Oil" (see page 12). This section explains how the properties of the oil change when it comes into contact with heat. I explain the qualities of the different oils and which ones are best suited to various culinary uses. For example, extra-virgin olive oil, the best-quality oil, should be reserved for use as a condiment, when its intense flavor can be savored.

There are parallels between wine making and olive-oil production. Like a fine wine, a superior olive oil should be admired and cherished. Fortunately, unlike many fine wines, there is no advantage in allowing an olive oil to mature; it can be used as soon as it is bottled. All olive oil should be stored in a cool, dark place but not in the refrigerator. If these guidelines are followed, an oil should keep fresh for up to a year, but if you use it as much as I do it will be consumed long before that!

Introduction

Although the exact date and origin of the first olive tree is unknown, it is generally accepted to have been first cultivated in the Middle East and Crete as far back as the year 3000 B.C., possibly even earlier. Olive oil is produced from the fruit of the olive tree, *Olea europea*. Not only valuable in culinary terms, the oil was used in ancient times as an anointment for the body and hair, as a healing ointment, in both the making of terracotta lamps and as the fuel to light them. With such prolific qualities, the tree and its subsequent oil became an important source of income. Trade saw widespread growth of the trees throughout the Mediterranean.

ABOVE: Olive groves thrive in a Mediterranean climate

The Tree

Olive trees were first introduced to France and Italy by the ancient Greeks. The trees spread through the Roman Empire as it expanded. The Greeks also took them into Spain, and in the 16th century, the Spanish, on their own travels westward, were responsible for introducing this native Mediterranean tree to the countries of North and South America and the West Indies. Today the olive tree can be found in almost any country where the growing conditions suit it. It thrives in the Mediterranean and countries of similar climate–mild winters, a brief wet spring and fall, with hot, dry summers. Although it can survive long droughts, it does not tolerate extreme cold or wet. It is able to thrive in poor, rocky soil where other crops cannot. The mountainous regions of Greece and Italy are ideal growing areas; as the trees require little attention, the limited access is not a problem.

Thomas Jefferson introduced the olive tree to his estate in Virginia in the 1770s, but the trees did not survive. When the Spanish brought the trees to California in the mid-1800s the conditions were more suitable and the crops flourished. Consequently, the small amount of olive oil produced in the United States comes from California.

The olive tree is an evergreen, characterized by its rather gnarled trunk and unruly branches. The thin spiky leaves are a dark green on top with a silver scaly underside, and they live for about three years before being replaced by new leaves. The tree bears fruit from five years but does not mature until twenty and can live for more than one hundred years. Even when the tree dies, shoots sprout up from the base, replacing the old trunk, eventually becoming new trees themselves.

Groups of white blossoms appear early in the year. About one in twenty actually produces an olive. A prolonged wet spell at this time can be disastrous. Fruition commences in June and continues until early October when the pit turns hard, the pulp fills out and it becomes the flesh of the pear – or drop-shaped fruit – the olive. Olives are harvested in late autumn and winter, depending on both the variety of the tree and whether the olive is for eating or for oil production. Green olives are harvested from October and black olives from November to February.

The Olive

The olive is a pit fruit and in terms of ripening, there is no difference between the many green and black varieties. Olives are always green when unripe and turn black as they ripen, with varying degrees of red, purple and brown in between.

Some varieties produce good eating olives, for example the black Greek *Kalamata* or the green Spanish *Manzanilla*. Others are grown specifically for their oil, such as the Italian *Frantoio* and the Spanish *Cornicaba*.

Different varieties of olive ripen at different times and although the percentage of oil increases as the fruit ripens, the color of the oil is determined by the variety, not necessarily the ripeness, of the fruit. Some produce a very green oil even when the fruit is fully ripe, others are only green when the olive is just ripe. The quality of the oil depends on the method of cultivation, harvesting, milling, climate and soil conditions, as well as the variety of olive. A good variety of olive will not produce a high-quality oil without the other determining factors.

Production

As yet, no machine has been invented to perfect the harvesting process and it is still mostly done by hand. Methods of harvesting vary from country to country.

ABOVE: *(clockwise from top left) A selection of olives: Spanish whole green, pitted Greek black, Gordal and Kalamata.*

The olives can be left to ripen until they fall from the trees, but more usually they are shaken off. Nets are often set a little above the ground to catch them and to prevent the heat in the soil causing the olives to ferment. Once gathered, the olives are taken to the mills for pressing. Firstly they are stored for several hours or up to three days which aids the release of the oil. Knowing how short or long a time to store the olives is crucial; if left in the heat for too long they will start to ferment and spoil. The method of production varies both regionally and nationally. Today the majority of olive mills use machinery for pressing the olive, but in some parts of the Mediterranean more traditional methods prevail.

Once the grower has determind that the olives are fit to press, they are washed and then crushed. The crushing extracts the oil. Traditionally, this was done by large stone wheels; today stainless-steel crushers are used to simultaneously crush, shear and rub the olives. They

ABOVE: Harvesting olives by hand in Greece.

are then ground to form a paste; this is spread out on fiber mats, piled one on top of the other and placed in a vertical press. A small amount of pressure is then exerted to extract the oil. This extraction method is called "cold pressing" or the first pressing of the oil. Modern equipment is increasingly being used to extract the oil. Olives are placed in a revolving machine that forces the oil from the crushed fruit.

Water is separated from the oil and the still-cloudy oil is transferred to large containers, or amphorae, where it is kept until spring. As the temperature starts to rise, the oil thins, leaving the cloudy sediment at the bottom. The clear premium oil, the extra-virgin olive oil, can then be filtered off. The quality of an oil is determined by the level of acidity; the higher the acidity the lower the quality. Extra-virgin olive oil must have an acidity level of less than one percent. About 90 percent of oil extracted in the "cold pressing" is extra-virgin.

The average worldwide production of olive oil is approximately two million tons, with about 90 percent of that produced by Mediterranean countries. Spain and Italy are the largest producers, followed by Greece, Tunisia, Turkey, Portugal, Morocco, Syria and France. The rest comes from the Middle East and the Americas.

Nutrition
Polyunsaturated fats have long been considered healthier than saturated fats, but recent research has found that monounsaturated fats, such as oleic acid, to be healthier still. Olive oil contains 80 percent oleic acid and a lower percentage of linoleic acid, a polyunsaturate. Research indicates that oleic acid is effective in reducing the amount of plasma cholesterol, responsible for the high level of heart disease. Olive oil is beneficial for maintaining a low cholesterol level, and the rate of heart disease is lower in countries where olive oil is consumed daily. Research has also suggested that olive oil has further benefits. It contains Vitamin A and this, along with the high percentage of oleic acid, stimulates bone growth. Olive oil is believed to be calming on the stomach, reducing acid and the risk of stomach ulcers. It also reduces the chance of constipation by aiding the passage of foods through the intestine and bowel. Olive oil stimulates the secretion of bile in the gall bladder which can help prevent gallstones. When olive oil is used as the main source of dietary fat, it appears to be healthier than saturated fats.

Types of Olive Oil
Olive varieties differ both from country to country and regionally. The label on a bottle of olive oil will state the grade of the oil, the level of acidity, country of origin, volume, and producer's name. "First pressing" or "cold pressing" can be seen on some bottles of extra-virgin olive oil and if the bottle comes from a single estate then the grower's name will also be listed. This is only usually the case with oil produced by a small grower.

Italian olive oil

It is generally accepted that Italy, especially Tuscany, produces some of the finest oils in the world. The main varieties of olives are *Corantina, Cerasolo, Frantoio, Leccino* and *Moriolo*. The main characteristics of an Italian oil is a deep green color and a peppery aftertaste. Many of the best oils come from single estates, although there are also cooperatives producing some fine oils.

Spanish olive oil

The main Spanish varieties are *Cornicabra, Hojiblanca, Manzanilla, Picual* and *Picudo*. Pale in color, Spanish oil tends to be a golden-yellow with a heavy taste of the sun and many also have a slight peppery taste. The Spanish oils tend to be more readily acceptable to a palate used to vegetable oils because they are less pronounced than many of the Italian oils.

Greek olive oil

Unlike other countries, there are many small growers in Greece, who send their annual olive crop to large co-operatives to be milled. Greek oils tend to be green in color and are generally good quality, although they frequently lack the superior flavor of Italian and Spanish olive oils.

French olive oil

A relatively small producer of olive oil, France, southern France in particular, produces some fine oils. Far paler in color and lighter in flavor, French oils possess a subtlety that oils from more southerly countries lack.

RIGHT: Olive oil must be labelled with the level of acidity, the grade of oil, the volume, the country of origin and the name of the producer.

Choosing Olive Oil

In recent years the interest and demand for olive oil has increased enormously. Subsequently, a wider selection of oils are available in stores. This is a good thing, but can be confusing. Presented with shelves of different oils from numerous countries of varying quality is enough to send many of us running for cover, but with a small amount of knowledge (and confidence) it is easy to make a sensible choice.

Supermarket brands are probably the first olive oil that many people buy and branded extra-virgin olive oil is sold at very reasonable prices. Unfortunately, these oils are often mediocre quality and are a typical example of oils from different countries, blended together, to produce a cheaper oil. On the other hand, single-estate oils are the best quality. Although they are expensive, it is money well spent. For anyone who is interested in cooking and enjoys good food, a superior bottle of single-estate extra-virgin olive oil is an essential ingredient to those in the cupboard.

Flavored oils have been infused with either herbs, garlic, chilies or citrus peels. Some brands are infused at the pressing stage, where lemons are actually pressed with the olives. Other methods of flavoring are added at a later stage. Most commonly this is done with a chemically produced essence added at the bottling stage. For homemade oil infusions, see page 14.

There are plenty of oils whch are neither the supermarket variety or from single estates. The only way to decide which oils you particularly like is to begin tasting. Some specialist stores and delicatessens hold tastings from time to time. Anyone interested in experimenting with olive oil should seek out these tastings. Start with oil from a particular country, become familar with the flavors, then go on to experiment with oils from different regions and growers.

ABOVE: Flavored oils.

Cooking with Olive Oil

Unlike many culinary oils, such as vegetable and sunflower, which are designed to have little or no flavor, olive oil is specifically produced with a pronounced olive flavor. But there are times when using an extra-virgin olive oil is impractical and pointless. Oils break down at high cooking temperatures and even at lower temperatures there is a certain amount of flavor loss.

Keep two or three different oils in your kitchen cupboard at one time. Use a single-estate extra-virgin olive oil to drizzle over salads and vegetable dishes, a good-quality extra-virgin olive oil for low-temperature cooking and finally a good-quality olive oil for cooking at higher temperatures, for baking, and for making mayonnaise and herb infusions.

Extra-Virgin Olive Oil
This expensive oil has a rich, deep flavor. It is best used as a flavoring in its own right. The Italians use it as a sauce to pour over grilled, broiled or poached fish and meat. It is excellent for salad dressings (although a fine oil should be reserved to pour neat over raw vegetable dishes) and is added to soups and stews as a condiment.

Virgin Olive Oil
Called either pure olive oil or, more commonly, olive oil, this is best used for cooking, providing the temperature is not too high. It is ideal for braising meat, fish and vegetables and should be used whenever a recipe calls for olive oil. Its lack of astringency makes it the preferred olive oil for baking cakes and cookies. French olive oil is particularly good for making mayonnaise as it does not overpower the flavor of the other ingredients.

Salad Dressings
Usually a salad dressing refers to a combination of oil, vinegar, salt, pepper with perhaps the addition of herbs, but numerous variations are possible. The ratio of oil to vinegar depends on personal preference, so it is best to experiment with the following dressings.

Vinaigrette

Add a little crushed garlic or 1 tablespoon chopped fresh herbs to this classic dressing, if wished. Store in the refrigerator for up to 5 days.

1 teaspoon DIJON MUSTARD
PINCH SUGAR
2 teaspoons WHITE-OR RED-WINE VINEGAR
6 tablespoons EXTRA-VIRGIN OLIVE OIL

Blend the mustard, sugar, vinegar and some salt and pepper together until combined. Gradually beat in the oil until it thickens. Use immediately or refrigerate in a screwtop jar. Shake well before use.

Citrus Oil Dressing

Use lemon-flavored oils for salads with tomatoes, lime-flavored oil with fish, or orange-flavored oil with vegetable salads such as fennel or beets.

2 teaspoons WHOLEGRAIN MUSTARD
2 teaspoons RASPBERRY VINEGAR
1/2 teaspoon HONEY
6 tablespoons CITRUS OIL (SEE PAGE 16)

Blend the mustard, vinegar, honey and some salt and pepper together. Gradually beat until thick.

Creamy Salad Dressing

1 tablespoon RED-OR WHITE-WINE VINEGAR
PINCH SUGAR
4 tablespoons EXTRA-VIRGIN OLIVE OIL
2 tablespoons WHIPPING CREAM

Blend the vinegar, sugar and some salt and pepper together until combined. Beat in the oil and cream until the dressing thickens. Use immediately or store in the refrigerator for 2-3 days. Serve at room temperature.

Oriental Salad Dressing

Use olive oil for this dressing to enhance the flavors of the other ingredients.

2 teaspoons RICE WINE OR SHERRY VINEGAR
1 tablespoon LIGHT SOY SAUCE
1 SMALL CLOVE GARLIC, CRUSHED
1/2 teaspoon GRATED FRESH GINGER ROOT
PINCH SUGAR
PEPPER
6 tablespoons OLIVE OIL
1 tablespoon SESAME OIL

Blend the vinegar, soy sauce, garlic, ginger, sugar and pepper together until combined. Gradually beat in the oils until they thicken. Use immediately or refrigerate and use as required.

Warm Salad Dressing

This can be poured over hearty salads that will stand up to the heat of the dressing and is particularly good with fish and shellfish salads.

6 tablespoons EXTRA-VIRGIN OLIVE OIL
1 teaspoon GRATED LEMON PEEL
1 CLOVE GARLIC, SLICED
1 tablespoon CAPERS, DRAINED AND CHOPPED
1 tablespoon BALSAMIC VINEGAR

Heat 2 tablespoons of the oil in a small pan and gently fry the lemon peel, garlic and capers for 3 minutes until softened. Stir in the vinegar, remove the pan from the heat and gradually beat in the remaining oil. Pour over the salad and serve immediately.

OIL INFUSIONS, SAUCES, PASTES AND PRESERVES

Oils infused with herbs, garlic, chilies or citrus peel add flavor to salad dressings, sauces and soups. Freshly made pastes add finesse to pasta, or can simply be spread on toast. Recipes containing fresh ingredients should be refrigerated and consumed within 5 days.

Raw Garlic Oil

Do not leave raw garlic in oil for more than 2 weeks because it can spoil and taint the oil.

2 cloves GARLIC

1/2 teaspoon SALT

1 1/4 cups OLIVE OIL

Crush the garlic and salt together, using a mortar and pestle or on a chopping board. Place in a clean jar. Pour in the oil, seal and store overnight. Use as required for up to 2 weeks.

MAKES 1 1/4 CUPS

Caramelized Garlic Oil

Cook the garlic before infusing in fresh oil because the oil will keep for longer.

2 whole heads GARLIC

2/3 cup OLIVE OIL

Preheat the oven to 375°F. Peel the outer layers of the garlic heads and place them on a double layer of foil. Add 2 tablespoons of the oil, seal the packages and bake for 1 hour until the cloves are tender. Leave until cool. Transfer to a clean jar, add the remaining oil and seal. Leave to infuse in the refrigerator. Use within 5 days.

MAKES 2/3 CUP

TOP: Caramelized Garlic Oil
BOTTOM: Raw Garlic Oil

Citus Oils

Unwaxed citrus fruits are recommended. Alternatively, rinse and wipe the fruits well before peeling.

4 strips CITRUS PEEL (LEMON, LIME OR ORANGE)
1¹/₄ cups EXTRA-VIRGIN OLIVE OIL

Place the peel in a clean jar and pour the oil over. Store in a cool, dark place for up to 2 weeks. Strain into a clean jar. Use as required. MAKES 1¹/₄ CUPS

Wicked Chili Oil

A fiery oil, this is for lovers of hot spices.

1¹/₄ cups OLIVE OIL
2 tablespoons CHILI FLAKES OR CRUSHED RED CHILIES

Pour the oil into a clean jar, add the chili flakes and leave to infuse for several days. Use as required. MAKES 1¹/₄ CUPS

Olio Santo

A fairly mild chili infusion that adds a subtle heat to any dish.

4 whole DRIED RED CHILIES
8 BAY LEAVES, BRUISED
1¹/₄ cups EXTRA-VIRGIN OLIVE OIL

Rinse and dry the chilies and bay leaves and put in a clean jar. Pour in the oil, seal the jar and leave in a cool place for at least 3 weeks. Use as required. MAKES 1¹/₄ CUPS

Herb Oil

Rosemary, basil, tarragon, mint, parsley and chives all work well in oil infusions, either separately or mixed together.

1/2 ounce FRESH LEAVES OF CHOSEN HERBS
1¹/₄ cups OLIVE OIL

Lightly bruise the herbs by tapping them with a rolling pin. Put them in a clean jar. Add the oil, shake well so that the leaves fall to the bottom and are totally covered with oil. Store in a cool, dark place for at least 1 week and up to 4 weeks. Strain the oil into a clean jar. Use as required. MAKES 1¹/₄ CUPS

TOP: Citrus Oil, Wicked Chili Oil
BOTTOM: Herb Oil

Skordalià

❧

2 *slices* DAY-OLD WHITE BREAD, CUBED
4 *tablespoons* MILK
2 *cloves* GARLIC, CRUSHED
1/2 teaspoon SEA SALT
pinch CAYENNE PEPPER
6 *tablespoons* EXTRA-VIRGIN OLIVE OIL
1 *tablespoon* LEMON JUICE

Soak the bread in the milk for 5 minutes. Squeeze out the milk and put the bread in a blender or food processor. Add the garlic, salt and cayenne pepper and blend until smooth. Gradually blend in the oil and 1 tablespoon boiling water to form a thick sauce. Stir in the lemon juice and season to taste. Refrigerate and use within 2 days.

MAKES ABOUT 1 CUP

Aïoli

❧

4-8 *cloves* GARLIC
1/2 teaspoon SEA SALT
2 EGG YOLKS
1 *tablespoon* WHITE-WINE VINEGAR
1 1/4 cups OLIVE OIL

Crush the garlic cloves with the salt, then place in a bowl and stir in the egg yolks and vinegar. Gradually beat in the oil, a little at a time, beating well after each addition until thick and glossy. Season to taste and store in a clean jar in the refrigerator for up to 5 days.

MAKES ABOUT 1 1/4 CUPS

Mayonnaise

❧

2 EGG YOLKS
pinch SUGAR
1 *teaspoon* DIJON MUSTARD
1/4 teaspoon SEA SALT
FRESHLY GROUND BLACK PEPPER
1 *teaspoon* WHITE-WINE VINEGAR OR LEMON JUICE
1 *cup plus 1 tablespoon* OLIVE OIL

Put the egg yolks, sugar, mustard, salt, pepper and vinegar or lemon juice into a bowl. Beat until pale and creamy. Gradually beat in the oil, a little at a time, beating well after each addition until all the oil is incorporated. Adjust seasonings to taste. Thin the mayonnaise with a little boiling water if very thick and store in a clean jar. Keep refrigerated for up to 5 days.

MAKES ABOUT 1 1/4 CUPS

TOP: *Skordalià*
BOTTOM: *Mayonnaise*

Pesto

This classic Italian sauce, made with fresh basil, is traditionally served with pasta or as a condiment for soups.

1 clove GARLIC, CHOPPED
1/2 teaspoon SEA SALT
1/2 cup BASIL LEAVES
2 tablespoons PINE NUTS, TOASTED
1/2 cup EXTRA-VIRGIN OLIVE OIL
2 tablespoons FRESHLY GRATED PARMESAN CHEESE
FRESHLY GROUND BLACK PEPPER

Blend the garlic, salt, basil and pine nuts in a blender or food processor until fairly smooth. Transfer to a bowl. Stir in the olive oil, Parmesan and pepper until combined and season to taste. Store in a clean jar and refrigerate for up to 5 days.

For Red Pesto

Replace the pine nuts with 2 ounces drained sun-dried tomatoes in oil. Continue as above.

For Parsley Pesto

Replace the basil with parsley and add 2 tablespoons capers and 1 teaspoon grated lemon peel. Continue as above.

ALL MAKE ABOUT 2/3 CUP

Anchovy Paste

This seasoning or paste is based on anchoïade, *made in the south of France.*

2 x 2-oumce CANS ANCHOVIES IN OIL, DRAINED
MILK
1 clove GARLIC, CHOPPED
2 tablespoons CHOPPED FRESH BASIL
pinch CHILI FLAKES
1 tablespoon LEMON JUICE
2 tablespoons PINE NUTS
6 tablespoons EXTRA-VIRGIN OLIVE OIL

Soak the anchovies in a little milk for 10 minutes. Drain well and pat dry on paper towels. Put the anchovies in a blender or food processor with all the remaining ingredients, except the oil, and blend to form a fairly smooth paste. Gradually blend in the oil. Transfer to a clean jar and refrigerate for up to 5 days.

MAKES ABOUT 1 CUP

TOP: Pesto
BOTTOM: Anchovy Paste

OLIVE OIL

Therapeutic Effect: *Taken internally, olive oil stimulates metabolism, promotes digestion and lubricates mucous membranes. It can also be applied externally to treat dry skin.*

Components

Olive oil contains 77 percent monounsaturated fatty acids, 14 percent saturated fatty acids and 9 percent polyunsaturated fatty acids, plus vegetable mucilage and vitamin E.

Help for the digestive tract

Take 1 tbsp. of olive oil on an empty stomach to stimulate digestion and relieve upset stomach, flatulence and heartburn.

Olive oil for constipation

In the morning, take 1 tsp. of olive oil mixed with lemon juice on an empty stomach. Or try an enema made from 5 oz. of olive oil in 20 oz. of boiling water, cooled to lukewarm.

The antioxidant benefit

The vitamin E in olive oil is an antioxidant. In addition, monounsaturated fatty acids are less easily damaged by oxygen than other types of fat. They are therefore less likely to produce free radicals, which damage cell membranes and contribute to several diseases.

Extra Tip

To help build strong fingernails and soften cuticles, soak your nails each night in a mixture of 3 parts lukewarm olive oil to 1 part freshly-squeezed lemon juice. Put on cloth gloves and let the oil penetrate overnight. Your nails will gradually become more resistant to breaking and chipping.

*U*sed for cardiovascular diseases, high blood cholesterol, earaches, constipation, stomach upset, dry skin and stretch marks

Applications

◆ *To lower blood cholesterol levels*
The monounsaturated fatty acids in olive oil help lower LDL ("bad") cholesterol levels without affecting HDL ("good") cholesterol or triglyceride levels. To lower your cholesterol, at least 15 percent of your daily calories should come from monounsaturated fatty acids. Whenever possible, use olive oil in place of butter or other vegetable oils in cooking, in preparing dressings for salads or vegetables and in making sandwiches.

◆ *To treat ear complaints*
To clear stopped-up ears, put a few drops of lukewarm olive oil in the affected ear. Lie for 5 min. on the opposite side, then turn over, so that the olive oil can flow out again. (Do not put any liquid in your ear if you think you may have a perforated eardrum!) For earaches, soak a cotton pad in olive oil, then add 5 drops of lavender oil. Place it loosely in your outer ear until the pain abates.

◆ *To prevent hair loss*
Massage the scalp with olive oil every evening for eight days. Let it work overnight and wash it out in the morning.

◆ *To moisturize skin*
Apply daily to dry spots or stretch marks.

148 20046 1201 B

The Complete Guide to Natural Healing makes every effort to provide medically accurate and up-to-date information that is intended to complement, not replace, the advice of your physician. Before undertaking the advice contained in this publication, you should consult with a health care professional, who can best assess your individual needs, symptoms and treatment.

©MCMXCIX International Masters Publishers AB. The Complete Guide to Natural Healing ™ IMP AB, produced under license by IMP Inc.
Pkt. 00   Printed in USA

NATURE'S REMEDIES

Olive Oil

Although the olive tree originated in Asia, it has been cultivated for over 3,000 years in Mediterranean countries, where much of the olive crop is used to make olive oil. In this process, olives are pitted and ground to a thick pulp. The pulp is then pressed to remove the juices, which are placed in a centrifuge to separate the water from the oil. One tablespoon of olive oil contains 120 calories and 14 grams of fat, but the fat is mostly monounsaturated; it has a beneficial effect on blood cholesterol levels and is easily digested. In those countries where olive oil is consumed extensively, such as Greece, Italy and Spain, there is a low incidence of cardiovascular diseases. The mild vegetable mucilage in olive oil protects the body's digestive tract. Ancient civilizations used olive oil to help heal wounds. Today, it is considered a good remedy for skin problems and an effective moisturizer.

CHOOSE THE HIGHEST QUALITY OLIVE OIL

Use only olive oil that is labeled "extra virgin." This guarantees that the oil has been cold-pressed from freshly harvested olives and does not contain chemicals. Extra virgin olive oil supplies the best flavor and oil that is golden-yellow in color is of higher quality than green.

Harissa Paste

A spicy Moroccon paste which can be added to stews. Use sparingly as the chilies make it very hot.

2 ounces DRIED RED CHILIES, SEEDED
2 large cloves GARLIC, CHOPPED
1/4 teaspoon SEA SALT
1/3 cup EXTRA-VIRGIN OLIVE OIL

Put the chilies in a bowl and cover with warm water. Leave to soak for 1 hour. Drain well and place in a blender or food procesor with the garlic and salt. Blend until fairly smooth, then gradually blend in the oil to form a smooth paste. Place in a clean jar and store in a refrigerator for up to 5 days.   MAKES ABOUT 1/2 CUP

Walnut Paste

Stir into freshly cooked pasta for a quick-and-simple supper dish.

1 cup WALNUTS, TOASTED
1 small bunch SCALLIONS, TRIMMED AND CHOPPED
2 cloves GARLIC
2 tablespoons CHOPPED FRESH BASIL OR PARSLEY
6 tablespoons EXTRA-VIRGIN OLIVE OIL

Place all the ingredients, except the oil, in a blender or food processor and blend until fairly smooth. Gradually add the oil until combined. Place in a clean jar and refrigerate for up to 5 days.   MAKES ABOUT 2/3 CUP

Tapenade

A thick, rich olive paste, ideal for pizzas, pasta dishes or on toast.

1 ounce ANCHOVIES IN OIL, DRAINED
MILK
1 cup PITTED RIPE OLIVES
2 tablespoons CAPERS IN BRINE, DRAINED
1 clove GARLIC, CHOPPED
1 tablespoon CHOPPED FRESH PARSLEY
1 teaspoon GRATED LEMON PEEL
1 tablespoon WHITE-WINE VINEGAR
6 tablespoons EXTRA-VIRGIN OLIVE OIL

Soak the anchovies in a little milk for 10 minutes. Drain well and pat dry. Put the anchovies and all the remaining ingredients, except the oil, in a blender or food processor and blend to form a smooth paste. Blend in the oil and transfer to a clean jar. Refrigerate for up to 5 days.   MAKES ABOUT 1 CUP

TOP: *Harissa Paste*
BOTTOM: *Tapenade*

Fragrant Olives

❦

1¹/₂ teaspoons FENNEL SEEDS
1 cup GREEN OLIVES
1 cup RIPE OLIVES
1 clove GARLIC, SLICED
1 teaspoon PINK PEPPERCORNS, LIGHTLY CRUSHED
1 tablespoon GRATED ORANGE PEEL
1 tablespoon ORANGE JUICE
1 RED CHILI, SEEDED AND CHOPPED
4 tablespoons EXTRA-VIRGIN OLIVE OIL

Toast the fennel seeds and lightly crush them. Place all the ingredients in a bowl, stir well. Cover and leave to marinate. Keep refrigerated and use within 1-2 days.

MAKES ABOUT 2 CUPS

Dried and Preserved Cherry Tomatoes

❦

Drying tomatoes in the oven is the nearest equivalent to those dried naturally in the sun, and the result is surprisingly good.

2 pounds CHERRY TOMATOES, STEMS REMOVED
SEA SALT
1 tablespoon FENNEL SEEDS
2 dried RED CHILIES
EXTRA-VIRGIN OLIVE OIL, TO COVER

Preheat the oven to 225°F. Rinse the tomatoes carefully and dry well on paper towels. Halve the tomatoes and lay, cut sides up, on large baking sheets. Sprinkle a little sea salt over and bake for 6-7 hours, turning them half way through, until they are shriveled and dried out. Cool on a wire a rack until completely cool. Pour boiling water over, soak for 10 minutes, drain and dry thoroughly. Store in a jar with the fennel seeds, chilies and enough oil to completely cover them.

MAKES ABOUT 2 POUNDS

Marinated Olives

❦

8 ounces RIPE OLIVES
2 cloves GARLIC, LIGHTLY POUNDED
2 BAY LEAVES
4 dried RED CHILIES
2 strips LEMON PEEL
1 tablespoon CHOPPED FRESH THYME
1 ¹/₂ teaspoons CUMIN SEEDS, TOASTED
1 teaspoon BLACK PEPPERCORNS, BRUISED
2 tablespoons RED-WINE VINEGAR
EXTRA-VIRGIN OLIVE OIL, TO COVER

Arrange the olives, garlic, bay leaves, chilies, lemon peel, thyme, cumin seeds and peppercorns in a clean jar. Mix the vinegar with 2 tablespoons water. Pour into the jar with enough oil to completely cover the ingredients. Shake gently and then store in the refrigerator for several days.Use within 5 days.

MAKES ABOUT 1¹/₂ CUPS

TOP: Fragrant Olives, Dried and Preserved Cherry Tomatoes
BOTTOM: Marinated Olives

Soups and Appetizers

Drizzle extra-virgin olive oil over soups just before serving – the hot soup
brings out the flavor of the oil. Many of these appetizers require pastes, oil infusions
or sauces that have to be made ahead, so check the ingredients before beginning.

Soupe de Poisson

This classic French soup is served topped with croutons and rouille *– a fiery garlic and chili mayonnaise.*

1 pound LARGE RAW SHRIMP WITH SHELLS

1/2 ONION, CHOPPED

1 clove GARLIC

2 sprigs FRESH THYME

1 stalk CELERY, CHOPPED

6 1/4 cups FISH OR VEGETABLE STOCK

pinch SAFFRON STRANDS

2 tablespoons OLIVE OIL

1 RED ONION, CHOPPED

2 cloves GARLIC, CHOPPED

2 teaspoons PAPRIKA

1/4 teaspoon CAYENNE PEPPER

4 RIPE PLUM TOMATOES, CHOPPED

2/3 cup DRY WHITE WINE

1 tablespoon TOMATO PASTE

1 pound SKINLESS WHITE FISH,
FILLETED AND CUBED

GRATED PARMESAN CHEESE AND
CROUTONS, TO GARNISH

Rouille

1/2 SMALL RED BELL PEPPER, SEEDED

2 cloves GARLIC, CHOPPED

2 SMALL FRESH RED CHILIES,
SEEDED AND CHOPPED

1 cup FRESH WHITE BREAD CRUMBS

1 teaspoon LEMON JUICE

1/2 cup EXTRA-VIRGIN OLIVE OIL

Shell the shrimp and place the heads and shells in a pan; reserve the flesh. Add the onion, whole garlic clove, thyme, celery and stock to the shells and bring to a boil. Skim the surface to remove any scum, then cover and simmer gently for 30 minutes. Skim the surface again and strain the liquid into a measuring jug. Make up to 6 1/4 cups with water, if necessary, and stir in the saffron. Set aside to infuse for 10 minutes.

Meanwhile, prepare the rouille. Broil the pepper half for 6-8 minutes on each side until charred and tender. Transfer to a plastic bag. Cool. Peel, discard the skin and chop the flesh. Place in a blender or food processor with all the remaining *rouille* ingredients, except the oil. Add 2 tablespoons of the shrimp stock and blend to form a smooth paste. With the motor running, gradually blend in the oil through the feed tube until the sauce is thick and glossy. Refrigerate until required.

Heat the oil in a clean saucepan. Fry the onion, garlic, paprika and cayenne for 5 minutes until soft. Add the tomatoes and cook for 5 minutes longer. Add the wine, boil rapidly for 3 minutes, then stir in the tomato paste, saffron stock, fish and shrimp. Bring slowly to a boil, then cover and simmer gently for 20 minutes. Purée the soup until smooth and pass through a fine strainer into a clean pan. Heat through. Top with the *rouille*, cheese and croutons. Serve immediately. SERVES 6-8

RIGHT: Soupe de Poisson

Roasted Tomato Soup with Cilantro

2 pounds RIPE PLUM TOMATOES, QUARTERED
1/2 cup EXTRA-VIRGIN OLIVE OIL
1 tablespoon CHOPPED FRESH THYME
2 teaspoons GRATED LEMON PEEL
SEA SALT
1 LEEK, CHOPPED
2 cloves GARLIC, CHOPPED
1 tablespoon CORIANDER SEEDS, TOASTED AND CRUSHED
2/3 cup WHITE WINE
4 ounces STALE WHITE BREAD, CRUSTS REMOVED AND CRUMBLED
3 1/4 cups VEGETABLE STOCK
2 tablespoons CHOPPED FRESH CILANTRO
1 tablespoon LEMON JUICE

Preheat the oven to 450°F. Place the tomatoes in one layer on a large baking sheet. Drizzle 4 tablespoons olive oil over and sprinkle the thyme, lemon peel and some sea salt over. Roast for 30 minutes until the tomatoes are charred and very mushy.

Heat 2 tablespoons oil in a saucepan and fry the leek, garlic and coriander seeds for 5 minutes. Add the wine and boil for 3 minutes. Add the bread, tomatoes and stock. Bring to a boil, then cover and simmer for 20 minutes. Purée, then return to a clean pan to reheat. Blend the remaining oil, fresh cilantro and lemon juice together and drizzle over the soup.   SERVES 4

Potato and Garlic Soup with Arugula Pesto

2 heads GARLIC, CLOVES SEPARATED AND PEELED
5 cups VEGETABLE STOCK
1/2 teaspoon SEA SALT
1 BAY LEAF
2 sprigs FRESH PARSLEY
2 sprigs FRESH THYME

Soup
2 tablespoons OLIVE OIL
1 ONION, CHOPPED
1 teaspoon GROUND CUMIN
1 1/2 pounds FLOURY POTATOES, PEELED AND DICED

Arugula Pesto
2 ounces ARUGULA LEAVES
1 clove GARLIC, CHOPPED
1 tablespoon PINE NUTS
1 tablespoon FRESHLY GRATED PARMESAN CHEESE
4 tablespoons EXTRA-VIRGIN OLIVE OIL

Place the garlic cloves in a saucepan with the stock and salt. Tie the bay leaf and herbs in a piece of cheesecloth and add to the pan. Bring to a boil, then cover and simmer gently for 1 hour. Discard the cheesecloth bag and make the stock up to 5 cups with water, if necessary.

Heat the oil in a clean saucepan and fry the onion and cumin for 5 minutes until soft but not browned. Add the potatoes and fry for 5 minutes. Pour in the garlic broth and bring to a boil. Cover and simmer for 20 minutes until the potatoes are tender. Purée the soup until smooth. Season and return to the pan to heat through.

To make the arugula pesto, rinse and dry the arugula leaves and roughly chop. Place in a blender or food processor. Add the garlic, pine nuts and Parmesan and blend to form a fairly smooth paste. Gradually blend in the oil. Season to taste. Spoon the soup into bowls and stir in the pesto until well mixed.   SERVES 4-6

TOP: Roasted Tomato Soup with Cilantro
BOTTOM: Potato and Garlic Soup with Arugula Pesto

Lentil and Vegetable Broth with Anchovy Paste

3 tablespoons OLIVE OIL

1 ONION, CHOPPED

2 cloves GARLIC, CHOPPED

1 tablespoon CHOPPED FRESH ROSEMARY

2 CARROTS, DICED

1 POTATO, PEELED AND DICED

1 stalk CELERY, CHOPPED

1¹/₂ cups BROWN OR GREEN LENTILS

5 cups VEGETABLE OR CHICKEN STOCK

1¹/₄ cups TOMATO JUICE

2 BAY LEAVES

1 cup BROCCOLI FLOWERETS, CHOPPED

1 cup CAULIFLOWER FLOWERETS, CHOPPED

4 tablespoons ANCHOVY PASTE (SEE PAGE 20)

Heat the oil in a saucepan and fry the onion, garlic and rosemary for 5 minutes. Add the carrots, potato and celery and fry for 10 minutes longer. Rinse the lentils, then add them plus the stock, tomato juice and bay leaves. Bring to a boil, then cover and simmer for 40 minutes until the lentils are tender.

Stir in the broccoli, cauliflower and anchovy paste, return to the boil and simmer gently for 10 minutes until the vegetables are cooked. Adjust the seasoning. Serve immediately.   SERVES 6

Chilled Catalan Gazpacho

¹/₂ SMALL CUCUMBER, SEEDED AND CHOPPED

1 bunch SCALLIONS, TRIMMED AND CHOPPED

1 SMALL GREEN BELL PEPPER, SEEDED AND DICED

1 SMALL FRESH GREEN CHILI, SEEDED AND CHOPPED

2 RIPE TOMATOES, PEELED, SEEDED AND DICED

2 tablespoons CHOPPED FRESH PARSLEY

2 tablespoons CAPERS, PLUS EXTRA TO GARNISH

¹/₂ cup BLANCHED ALMONDS, FINELY GROUND

¹/₂ cup FRESH WHITE BREAD CRUMBS

¹/₂ teaspoon SUGAR

¹/₂ teaspoon SEA SALT

3 tablespoons WHITE-WINE VINEGAR

2¹/₂ cups COLD VEGETABLE STOCK

6 tablespoons EXTRA-VIRGIN OLIVE OIL

²/₃ cup ICED WATER

SALT AND PEPPER

Reserve a little cucumber and scallions. Place the remaining ingredients, except the stock, oil and water, in a blender or food processor and blend until fairly smooth. Gradually blend in the stock, oil and water until they are combined. Adjust the seasoning and chill for at least 1 hour.

Serve each portion topped with a couple of ice cubes, the reserved cucumber and scallions, a few extra capers and a drizzle of olive oil.   SERVES 4

RIGHT: Chilled Catalan Gazpacho

Mussel Soup with Charmoula

Charmoula Spice Mixture

1 teaspoon PAPRIKA
1/2 teaspoon GROUND CUMIN
1/2 teaspoon TURMERIC
1/4 teaspoon CAYENNE PEPPER
2 cloves GARLIC, CHOPPED
2 tablespoons CHOPPED FRESH CILANTRO
1 tablespoon LEMON OR LIME JUICE
4 tablespoons EXTRA-VIRGIN OLIVE OIL

Soup

3 pounds FRESH MUSSELS
pinch SAFFRON STRANDS
2 tablespoons OLIVE OIL
1 RED ONION, CHOPPED
2 teaspoons CHOPPED FRESH THYME
4 TOMATOES, CHOPPED
2 tablespoons TOMATO PASTE
3 3/4 cups FISH OR VEGETABLE STOCK

Place all the ingredients for the charmoula in a blender or food processor and blend to form a rough paste. Set aside. Scrub the mussels well and rinse well under cold water. Discard any that remain open when tapped. Place in a large saucepan. Cover and cook over medium heat for 5 minutes, shaking the pan occasionally, until all the shells have opened. Discard any closed mussels. Strain the liquid through a fine strainer and stir in the saffron. Carefully shell the mussels. Reserve.

Heat the oil in a clean saucepan and fry the onion and thyme for 5 minutes. Stir in all but 2 tablespoons of the charmoula and fry gently for 5 minutes longer. Add the remaining ingredients. Bring to a boil, then cover and simmer for 20 minutes. Add all but a few mussels and simmer for 10 minutes longer. Purée until fairly smooth. Return to the pan, add the reserved mussels and heat through. Garnish with the reserved charmoula.

SERVES 4

Turkish-Style Oven Soup

1/3 cup DRIED GARBANZO BEANS, SOAKED
OVERNIGHT AND DRAINED
1/3 cup DRIED NAVY BEANS, SOAKED OVERNIGHT
AND DRAINED
1/2 cup BULGUR WHEAT
4 ounces BONELESS LAMB, CUBED
4 tablespoons OLIVE OIL
1 ONION, CHOPPED
2 CARROTS, DICED
1 tablespoon CHOPPED FRESH MINT
1 tablespoon DRIED OREGANO
2 TOMATOES, DICED
4 whole RED CHILIES
1 teaspoon each GROUND CUMIN, CORIANDER
AND CINNAMON
5 cups BEEF STOCK
EXTRA-VIRGIN OLIVE OIL AND PARSLEY

Preheat the oven to 350°F. Place all the ingredients into a large clay pot or casserole, add salt if wished, and cover with a tight-fitting lid. Bake for 2-2 1/2 hours or until the beans, vegetables and meat are tender. Check from time to time to ensure the soup does not dry out and add extra stock if necessary.

Serve the soup straight from the pot or casserole, garnished with the olive oil and the parsley, and pass round some Mediterranean bread (see page 90).

SERVES 6-8

TOP: Mussel Soup with Charmoula
BOTTOM: Turkish-Style Oven Soup

Broiled Field Mushrooms with Rosemary Aïoli

1/2 quantity AÏOLI (SEE PAGE 18)
1 tablespoon CHOPPED FRESH ROSEMARY NEEDLES
4 LARGE FIELD MUSHROOMS
OLIVE OIL FOR BRUSHING
2 ENGLISH MUFFINS
1/2 quantity CARAMELIZED ONIONS (SEE PAGE 36)

Make up a half quantity of aïoli according to the recipe on page 18, adding the rosemary to the egg yolks and vinegar. Cover and set aside. Wipe the mushrooms with a damp cloth and cut away and discard the stems. Brush with oil and place on a broiler rack. Broil for 5-6 minutes on each side until golden and tender.

Split and toast the muffins. Spread a little rosemary aïoli over each half, top with a mushroom, a little more aïoli and finish with a spoonful of caramelized onions. Serve immediately. SERVES 4

Smoked Salmon Blinis with Chive Oil

1 3/4 cups ALL-PURPOSE FLOUR
1/4 teaspoon SALT
1 teaspoon RAPID-RISE ACTIVE-DRY YEAST
1 cup MILK, WARMED
2 EGGS
3 tablespoons EXTRA-VIRGIN OLIVE OIL
1 tablespoon SNIPPED FRESH CHIVES
1/2 cup LIME CITRUS OIL (SEE PAGE 16)
EXTRA OLIVE OIL FOR BRUSHING
8 ounces SMOKED SALMON
CRÈME FRAÎCHE OR SOUR CREAM,
TO SERVE

Sift the flour and salt into a bowl. Stir in the yeast. Gradually beat in the milk until smooth. Cover and leave in a warm place for 30 minutes until frothy. Beat the eggs and beat into the yeast mixture with the olive oil. Cover and set aside for 30 minutes. Gently pound the chives and stir into the lime oil. Set aside.

Brush a large nonstick skillet with oil and place over medium heat. When hot, pour 4 spoonfuls of the yeast mixture into the pan to form small pancakes. Cook for 2-3 minutes until the undersides are golden and holes appear on the tops, then flip over with a spatula or pancake turner and cook for 1 minute longer until browned on each side. Keep warm and repeat to make 16 blinis. Top with smoked salmon and crème fraîche. Drizzle with chive oil and serve immediately. SERVES 8

RIGHT: Smoked Salmon Blinis with Chive Oil

Bruschetta

❦

4 THICK SLICES FRENCH BREAD

2 cloves GARLIC

EXTRA-VIRGIN OLIVE OIL

Toast the bread on both sides over a barbecue or under a broiler. While still hot rub both sides all over with garlic. Quickly drizzle with oil. Serve immediately.

SERVES 4

Chicken Liver and Arugula Bruschetta

❦

1 quantity BRUSCHETTA (SEE ABOVE)

3 tablespoons OLIVE OIL

1 SHALLOT, FINELY CHOPPED

1 clove GARLIC, CHOPPED

1 teaspoon CHOPPED FRESH THYME

8 ounces CHICKEN LIVERS, RINSED AND DRIED

2 tablespoons RED WINE

2 ounces ARUGULA LEAVES

1 teaspoon BALSAMIC VINEGAR

Prepare some bruschetta as above. Keep warm while frying the chicken livers. Heat 2 tablespoons oil in a small skillet and fry the shallot, garlic and thyme for 3 minutes. Increase the heat and add the chicken livers. Stir-fry for 3-4 minutes. Add the wine, then remove the pan from the heat. Meanwhile, toss the arugula leaves with the remaining oil and the vinegar. Arrange on top of the bruschetta. Add the chicken livers and serve.

SERVES 4

Anchovy, Caramelized Onion and Radicchio Bruschetta

❦

1 tablespoon OLIVE OIL

1 tablespoon BUTTER

4 SMALL RED ONIONS, CUT INTO WEDGES

2 teaspoons CHOPPED FRESH ROSEMARY NEEDLES

2 teaspoons BROWN SUGAR

2 tablespoons VINEGAR

1 quantity BRUSCHETTA (SEE ABOVE)

1 1/2 tablespoons ANCHOVY PASTE (SEE PAGE 20)

1 head RADICCHIO

EXTRA-VIRGIN OLIVE OIL

Heat the oil and butter in a small skillet. Fry the onions for 5 minutes. Cover and cook over low heat for 20 minutes until caramelized. Add the rosemary, sugar and vinegar and cook for 5 minutes longer. Keep warm. Prepare the bruschetta as above. Brush each one with a little anchovy paste and keep warm.

Cut the radicchio lengthwise into 4 slices, brush with oil and broil for 2-3 minutes on each side until lightly charred. Arrange over the bruschetta and top with the caramelized onions.

SERVES 4

RIGHT: *Bruschetta*

Eggplant Dip

2 medium EGGPLANTS

2 cloves GARLIC, CRUSHED

1/2 teaspoon SEA SALT

juice of 1/2 LEMON

2 tablespoons CHOPPED FRESH CILANTRO

pinch CAYENNE PEPPER

6 tablespoons EXTRA-VIRGIN OLIVE OIL

CHOPPED FRESH CILANTRO, TO GARNISH

Preheat the oven to 400°F. Wipe the eggplants, prick them all over with a fork and bake for 1 hour until the flesh feels soft. Cool. Peel and discard the skin, mash the flesh and strain in a strainer to extract all the excess liquid. Transfer to a blender or food processor. Add the garlic, salt, lemon juice, cilantro and cayenne and blend until fairly smooth. Gradually beat in the oil. Season to taste.

Cover and leave to marinate for several hours. Top with a little cilantro and an extra drizzle of olive oil. Serve with bread, toast or a selection of vegetable crudités.

SERVES 6-8

Warm Butter Bean and Sage Pâté

This fragrant pâté can be served warm as an appetizer, but it is just as good cold with bread or vegetable crudités. Look for imported butter beans in specialty gourmet stores; they have a rich, buttery taste. If you can't find any, substitute canned lima or fava beans.

4 tablespoons OLIVE OIL

1/2 SMALL ONION, FINELY CHOPPED

1 clove GARLIC, CHOPPED

1 tablespoon CHOPPED FRESH SAGE

1 teaspoon GRATED LEMON PEEL

1 x 14-ounce CAN BUTTER BEANS

1 teaspoon LEMON JUICE

pinch CAYENNE PEPPER

EXTRA-VIRGIN OLIVE OIL, TO DRIZZLE

Heat the oil in a skillet and fry the onion, garlic, sage and lemon peel for 5 minutes until soft but not golden. Add the beans, with about 6 tablespoons of their liquid, the lemon juice and cayenne. Cover and simmer gently for 5 minutes. Mash the beans with a potato masher to form a rough paste. Season to taste. Spread on bruschetta (see page 36) and serve immediately, or transfer to a small bowl and serve cold, drizzled with extra oil.

SERVES 4-8

TOP: *Eggplant Dip*

BOTTOM: *Warm Butter Bean and Sage Pâté*

Whole Baked Garlic with Camembert

4 heads GARLIC
3/4 cup OLIVE OIL
4 sprigs FRESH THYME
4 ounces CAMEMBERT CHEESE

Preheat the oven to 375°F. Peel away the thick outer layer of skin from the garlic heads. Use a sharp knife to slice off about 1/4 inch from the top. Cut 4 double layers of foil and place a garlic head in the middle of each. Draw up the sides to form a bowl, add 2 tablespoons oil, a sprig of thyme and salt and pepper to each one. Seal the packages and bake for 40 minutes.

Open the packages. Add another 1 tablespoon oil to each. Re-seal the packages and bake for 15-20 minutes longer until the garlic is golden and soft. Serve each head with a slice of Camembert on toast or bread, with the extra juices from the package.   SERVES 4

Beef Carpaccio

8 ounces FILLET OF BEEF
SEA SALT
1/2 cup VERY THINLY SLICED FENNEL
slivers PARMESAN CHEESE

Dressing
1 tablespoon CAPERS IN BRINE, DRAINED AND
    FINELY CHOPPED
1 teaspoon GRATED LEMON PEEL
1 tablespoon CHOPPED FRESH PARSLEY
1 tablespoon CHOPPED FRESH BASIL
6 tablespoons EXTRA-VIRGIN OLIVE OIL
juice of 1/2 LEMON
    EXTRA LEMON JUICE, TO SERVE
    FRESHLY GROUND BLACK PEPPER

Freeze the beef fillet for about 15 minutes to help firm it up. Use a very sharp knife to cut the fillet into wafer-thin slices, sprinkle a little sea salt over and top with fennel and Parmesan.

Beat all the dressing ingredients together and pour over the beef. Cover loosely with plastic wrap and marinate at room temperature for 1 hour. Squeeze some extra lemon juice over, grind the black pepper over and serve immediately.   SERVES 4

TOP: *Whole Baked Garlic with Camembert*
BOTTOM: *Beef Carpaccio*

Seafood Dishes

This diverse collection of international recipes shows how widely olive oil is used in seafood cooking. Dishes range from a South American-style seviche of raw salmon to the sweet and savory Fish Couscous, a traditional North African stew.

Fish Couscous

2 pounds WHITE FISH FILLETS, CUBED
2 cups COUSCOUS

Spice Mix
1 tablespoon CORIANDER SEEDS, TOASTED
1 tablespoon CUMIN SEEDS, TOASTED
2 teaspoons GROUND CINNAMON
2 teaspoons TURMERIC
grated peel and juice of 1/2 LEMON
2 teaspoons HARISSA PASTE (SEE PAGE 22)
3 tablespoons EXTRA-VIRGIN OLIVE OIL

Stew
3 tablespoons OLIVE OIL
4 ounces BUTTON MUSHROOMS
1 LARGE ONION, ROUGHLY CHOPPED
2 cloves GARLIC, CHOPPED
1 tablespoon CHOPPED FRESH THYME
2 CARROTS, CHOPPED
2 cups PURÉED AND STRAINED TOMATOES
1 x 14-ounce CAN GARBANZO BEANS
1/3 cup RAISINS
1/2 cup CASHEW NUTS, TOASTED
2 tablespoons CHOPPED FRESH PARSLEY
SALT AND PEPPER

Rinse and dry the fish. Set aside. Combine the ingredients for the spice mix and grind together to form a smooth paste. Toss 2 tablespoons with the cubed fish to coat. Marinate for several hours or overnight if possible.

Rinse the couscous with cold water and spread out over a large baking sheet. Pour 2 cups water over and leave to soak for 20 minutes.

To make the stew, heat 1 tablespoon of the oil in a large saucepan and fry the mushrooms for 3-4 minutes until golden. Remove with a slotted spoon. Add the remaining oil to the pan and fry the onion, garlic, thyme and carrots for 5 minutes. Add 1 tablespoon of the spice mix and fry for 5 minutes longer. Stir in the strained tomatoes and the garbanzo beans with their liquid and bring to a boil, then cover and simmer gently for 20 minutes.

Stir in the mushrooms, raisins and cashew nuts and carefully arrange the fish on top. Cover and simmer for 10 minutes longer until the fish flakes easily. Sprinkle the parsley over and season to taste. Meanwhile, steam the couscous, either over the stew in a double boiler, or in a cheesecloth-lined steamer for 8-10 minutes until fluffed up and tender. Spoon the couscous onto a serving dish and top with the stew. SERVES 4-6

RIGHT: Fish Couscous

Whole Sea Bream Baked in Paper

❦

Cooking fish in a paper packages seals in the flavors and steams the flesh, keeping the fish moist and tender.

1 x 12-ounce SEA BREAM, SCALED AND DRAWN

4 slices LEMON

4 sprigs FRESH PARSLEY

4 sprigs FRESH THYME

4 cloves GARLIC

SEA SALT

FRESHLY GROUND BLACK PEPPER

1 quantity RED PESTO (SEE PAGE 20)

EXTRA-VIRGIN OLIVE OIL FOR BRUSHING

Preheat the oven to 400°F. Rinse and dry the bream. Cut 4 slashes in the side of each fish. Place a slice of lemon, a sprig of each herb, a garlic clove and some salt and pepper into each body cavity. Spread each fish with the pesto.

Cut 4 large heart shapes out of parchment paper and make a fold line down the middle. Open the hearts out and brush with a little oil. Place a fish on one side of each heart and fold the other half over. Seal the edges to enclose the fish. Place on a large baking sheet and bake for 20 minutes. Let it stand for 5 minutes before serving straight from the paper packages. SERVES 4

New England Crab Cakes

❦

1 pound COOKED WHITE CRAB MEAT

2/3 cup MAYONNAISE (SEE PAGE 18)

2 cups FRESH WHITE BREAD CRUMBS

1 EGG, BEATEN

4 SCALLIONS, TRIMMED AND FINELY CHOPPED

2 teaspoons WORCESTERSHIRE SAUCE

1 teaspoon MUSTARD POWDER

1/2 teaspoon CAYENNE PEPPER

1/2 cup DRIED WHITE BREAD CRUMBS

VEGETABLE OIL FOR SHALLOW-FRYING

LEMON WEDGES AND EXTRA MAYONNAISE, TO SERVE

Fork through the crab meat, remove any small pieces of shell that may remain and discard. Place all the ingredients, except the dried bread crumbs, vegetable oil, lemon wedges and mayonnaise in a blender or food processor and blend to make a thick, rough paste. Chill for 1 hour. Form the mixture into 8 balls and carefully pat into flat cakes. Roll the cakes in the dried bread crumbs to coat well.

Heat about 1/2 inch vegetable oil in a skillet over medium heat and fry the cakes for 3-4 minutes on each side until golden and heated through. Serve immediately with lemon wedges and extra mayonnaise. SERVES 4

Top: Whole Sea Bream Baked in Paper

Bottom: New England Crab Cakes

Salmon Seviche with Corn Relish

12 ounces VERY FRESH SALMON FILLET
EXTRA OIL FOR BRUSHING

Marinade
6 tablespoons EXTRA-VIRGIN OLIVE OIL
grated peel and juice of 2 LIMES
pinch SUGAR
1 clove GARLIC, CRUSHED
2 SMALL FRESH CHILIES, SEEDED AND
CHOPPED
2 RIPE TOMATOES, PEELED, SEEDED AND
DICED

Relish
1 CORN COB
2 SCALLIONS, TRIMMED AND CHOPPED
2 tablespoons CRÈME FRAÎCHE OR SOUR CREAM
1 tablespoon LIME JUICE

Wash and dry the salmon and carefully pull out any remaining bones. Use a very sharp knife to slice the fish as thinly as possible. Place the salmon slices in a large nonmetallic shallow dish in a single layer. Combine all the marinade ingredients and pour over the salmon. Leave to marinate at room temperature for 1 hour. Strain off 2 tablespoons of the marinade and reserve.

Meanwhile, cook the corn in a pan of lightly salted boiling water for 5 minutes. Drain, refresh under cold water and pat dry. Brush the corn with oil and broil for 8-10 minutes, turning frequently until the kernels are tender and browned. Cool slightly. Cut the kernels away from the husk. Cool. Stir in the reserved marinade and the remaining ingredients. Season to taste. Serve the salmon with the relish. SERVES 4

Baked Mullet Niçoise

4 x 8-ounce RED MULLET, SCALED AND DRAWN

Sauce
4 tablespoons OLIVE OIL
1 SMALL EGGPLANT, DICED
1 ONION, CHOPPED
2 cloves GARLIC, CHOPPED
1 tablespoon CHOPPED FRESH THYME
1 tablespoon CHOPPED FRESH ROSEMARY NEEDLES
1 ZUCCHINI, DICED
1 RED BELL PEPPER, SEEDED AND DICED
2/3 cup RED WINE
3 cups PEELED AND CHOPPED RIPE PLUM
TOMATOES,
2/3 cup VEGETABLE STOCK
2 tablespoons TAPENADE (SEE PAGE 22)

Preheat the oven to 375°F. Rinse and dry the fish well. Set aside. Heat half the oil in a large skillet and fry the eggplant for 6-8 minutes until golden and tender. Remove with a slotted spoon and set aside. Add the remaining oil and fry the onion, garlic and herbs for 5 minutes. Add the zucchini and pepper and cook for 5 minutes longer. Return the eggplant to the pan, pour in the wine and boil rapidly for 5 minutes. Add the tomatoes, stock and tapenade and simmer gently for 15 minutes.

Pour half the sauce into the bottom of a baking dish and arrange the mullet in a single layer over the sauce. Top with the remaining sauce and bake for 20 minutes or until the fish flake easily if tested with a fork.

SERVES 4

RIGHT: Salmon Seviche with Corn Relish

Mixed Seafood Kebabs

❧

2 LEMONS

1 pound MONKFISH FILLET

1 pound HAKE, COD OR SALMON FILLET

16 JUMBO RAW SHRIMP OR TIGER PRAWNS

16 FRESH BAY LEAVES, SOAKED IN COLD
WATER FOR 20 MINUTES

Marinade

3/4 cup EXTRA-VIRGIN OLIVE OIL

1 cup DRY WHITE WINE

2 cloves GARLIC, CRUSHED

2 tablespoons CHOPPED FRESH CILANTRO

1 tablespoon CORIANDER SEEDS, ROASTED AND CRUSHED

Cut each lemon into 8 wedges. Rinse and dry the fish and cut each into large cubes. Wash and dry the shrimp. Alternately thread the lemon wedges, fish, shrimp and bay leaves onto 8 long skewers and place in a large nonmetallic, shallow dish. Combine the marinade ingredients. Pour over the skewered seafood. Cover and leave to marinate for as long as possible, preferably overnight.

Just before serving, preheat the broiler. Remove the kebabs from their marinade. Broil for 8-10 minutes, basting and turning frequently, until the fish and shrimp are firm to the touch. Bring any remaining marinade to a boil in a small pan. Serve the kebabs with the marinade drizzled over them.   SERVES 4

Chili Shrimp with Fennel Sauce

❧

24 JUMBO RAW SHRIMP OR TIGER PRAWNS

Marinade

1/2 cup WICKED CHILI OIL (SEE PAGE 16)

2 cloves GARLIC, CHOPPED

1 RED ONION, SLICED

1 RED CHILI, SEEDED AND CHOPPED

2 tablespoons CHOPPED FENNEL FRONDS

1 tablespoon CHOPPED FRESH THYME

Sauce

6 tablespoons EXTRA-VIRGIN OLIVE OIL

2 tablespoons BOILING WATER

2 tablespoons LEMON JUICE

2 cloves GARLIC, CRUSHED

2 tablespoons CHOPPED FENNEL FRONDS

Rinse and dry the shrimp and place them in a large nonmetallic, shallow dish. Combine all the marinade ingredients, except 2 tablespoons of the oil, and pour over the shrimp. Cover and refrigerate for several hours, preferably overnight.

Beat all the sauce ingredients together until thick. Remove the shrimp from their marinade and pat dry. Heat the reserved oil in a large skillet. Fry the shrimp over medium heat for 3-4 minutes until pink and golden. Add 4 tablespoons of the sauce. Cover and simmer for 3-4 minutes until the shrimp are cooked through. Serve hot with the remaining sauce.   SERVES 4

TOP: *Mixed Seafood Kebabs*

BOTTOM: *Chili Shrimp with Fennel Sauce*

Meat and Poultry Dishes

This chapter includes great traditional Mediterranean recipes like the Greek Souvlaki, where olive oil is used in the marinade as well as in the cooking of the lamb. The exotic chicken dishes are based on North African recipes.

Chicken with Preserved Lemon and Eggplants

Preserved lemons are available from Middle Eastern stores and some gourmet food stores. To preserve your own lemons, quarter 4 lemons, rub with sea salt and store for 2 weeks in a jar with 2 tablespoons sea salt and the juice of 4 lemons.

8 baby or 4 SMALL EGGPLANTS, HALVED LENGTHWISE
1 x 3 1/2 pounds CHICKEN

Stuffing
1/2 ONION
1 clove GARLIC
1/2 PRESERVED LEMON (SEE INTRODUCTION)
2 sprigs FRESH THYME
2 sprigs FRESH ROSEMARY

Stew
4 tablespoons OLIVE OIL
8 ounces PEARL ONIONS, HALVED
4 RIPE TOMATOES, CHOPPED
2/3 cup MEDIUM-DRY WHITE WINE
2/3 cup CHICKEN STOCK
2 tablespoons RED-WINE VINEGAR
3 tablespoons HONEY
2 PRESERVED LEMONS, ROUGHLY CHOPPED
4 sprigs FRESH ROSEMARY
2 tablespoons CHOPPED FRESH CILANTRO, TO GARNISH

Sprinkle the eggplants with salt. Drain in a colander for 30 minutes, then rinse well and dry thoroughly. Preheat the oven to 400°F.

Meanwhile, rinse and dry the chicken inside and out and place all the stuffing ingredients in the cavity. Truss up the chicken. Heat half the oil in a deep, nonstick skillet and fry the chicken to brown the skin all over. Transfer to a casserole and set aside.

For the stew, heat the oil and fry the onions in the skillet for 5 minutes until golden. Stir in the tomatoes, add the wine and boil rapidly for 5 minutes. Stir in the stock, vinegar and honey, then add to the casserole with the lemons and rosemary. Cover and bake for 30 minutes. Heat the remaining oil in the rinsed-out skillet and fry the eggplants for 5-6 minutes until golden. Add to the chicken, return to the oven and cook for 30-35 minutes longer until the chicken's leg juices run clear if pierced with a skewer and the vegetables are tender. Season to taste. Garnish with fresh cilantro.

SERVES 4

RIGHT: Chicken with Preserved Lemon and Eggplants

Souvlaki

Serve the tender chunks of marinated grilled or broiled lamb with Skordalià, the Greek version of mayonnaise (see page 18).

2 1/2 pounds NECK END OF LAMB
2 tablespoons CHOPPED FRESH ROSEMARY NEEDLES
1 tablespoon DRIED OREGANO
1 teaspoon DRIED MINT
1 ONION, CHOPPED
2 cloves GARLIC, CRUSHED
2 BAY LEAVES, BRUISED
1 1/4 cups RED WINE
4 tablespoons OLIVE OIL
1 quantity SKORDALIÀ, TO SERVE

Trim the excess fat from the lamb. Cut the lamb into large cubes and place in a large bowl. Combine all the remaining ingredients and toss with the lamb. Cover and marinate, for 12 hours or overnight, stirring from time to time.

Remove the lamb from its marinade and thread onto 4 long skewers. Cook over hot charcoals or under a hot broiler for 15-20 minutes, turning and basting frequently until the meat is charred on the outside but still slightly pink in the middle. Serve hot with lemon wedges and a bowl of skordalià.   SERVES 4

Chicken Tagine with Figs, Olives and Pistachio Nuts

8 LARGE DRIED FIGS
2/3 cup BOILING TEA
12 CHICKEN PIECES, SKINNED
1 quantity SPICE MIX (SEE PAGE 42)
4 tablespoons OLIVE OIL
6 ounces BUTTON MUSHROOMS, WIPED
1 LARGE ONION, ROUGHLY CHOPPED
2 LARGE CARROTS, THICKLY SLICED
2 cloves GARLIC, CRUSHED
2 teaspoons GRATED FRESH GINGER ROOT
1 cup CHICKEN STOCK
2 tablespoons TOMATO PASTE
1 tablespoon LEMON JUICE
1/3 cup PISTACHIO NUTS, SHELLED
1/3 cup PITTED RIPE OLIVES
2 tablespoons CHOPPED FRESH PARSLEY
HARISSA PASTE (PAGE 22), TO SERVE

Place the figs in a bowl, pour the tea over and leave to soak for 1 hour. Strain and reserve the liquid and chop the figs. Wash and dry the chicken pieces and toss with 4 tablespoons spice mix to coat.

Heat 1 tablespoon oil in a nonstick skillet and fry the mushrooms for 4-5 minutes until golden. Remove from the pan. Set aside. Heat the remaining oil and fry the spiced chicken over a high heat for 5-6 minutes until browned. Transfer to a flameproof casserole. Add the onion, carrots, garlic and ginger to the skillet and and fry for 10 minutes. Add the reserved fig liquid, chicken stock, tomato paste and lemon juice. Pour over the chicken and bring to a boil. Cover and simmer gently for 30 minutes. Add the figs, mushrooms, nuts and olives. Cover and simmer for 20 minutes longer. Sprinkle the parsley over and serve with rice or couscous and the harissa paste.   SERVES 4

RIGHT: Chicken Tagine with Figs and Nuts

Lamb Steaks with Beans

If you can't find cans of imported butter beans, substitute canned lima or fava beans.

3 tablespoons OLIVE OIL

4 LAMB STEAKS

1 x 4-ounce PIECE SLAB BACON, DICED

1 LARGE ONION, SLICED

2 cloves GARLIC, CHOPPED

1 tablespoon CHOPPED FRESH SAGE

2 RIPE TOMATOES, PEELED, SEEDED AND CHOPPED

6 tablespoons DRY WHITE WINE

2 x 14-ounce CANS BUTTER BEANS

1 tablespoon WHOLEGRAIN MUSTARD

Heat 2 tablespoons of the oil in a large nonstick skillet. Add the steaks and quickly fry over a high heat until both sides are well browned. Remove from the pan and keep warm. Add the bacon and fry for 5 minutes until golden. Add the onion, garlic and sage and continue to fry gently for 10 minutes.

Stir the tomatoes into the pan, add the wine and boil rapidly for 5 minutes. Drain the beans. Reserve 1¼ cups of their liquid. Add the mustard, beans and the liquid and boil, uncovered, for 15 minutes. Return the steaks to the pan. Cover and simmer gently for 6-8 minutes until the steaks are cooked through.   SERVES 4

Sausages Baked with Cabbage and Lentils

This rich and satisfying baked sausage dish is similar to cassoulet, a classic French dish. It is a great winter warmer and a good choice for a family supper.

1 cup PUY OR BROWN LENTILS

1¼ cups BEEF STOCK

4 tablespoons OLIVE OIL

8 SPICY ITALIAN SAUSAGES

1 ONION, CHOPPED

2 cloves GARLIC, CHOPPED

2 tablespoons CHOPPED FRESH SAGE

4 cups ROUGHLY SHREDDED SAVOY CABBAGE

3 cups PEELED, SEEDED AND DICED TOMATOES

2 tablespoons TOMATO PASTE

2 teaspoons CHILI SAUCE

Topping

4 tablespoons CHOPPED FRESH PARSLEY

¼ cup DRIED BREAD CRUMBS

2 tablespoons FRESHLY GRATED PARMESAN CHEESE

EXTRA OLIVE OIL

Rinse the lentils under cold running water for a few minutes and shake dry. Place in a saucepan, add plenty of cold water to cover them and bring to a boil. Cover and simmer for 30 minutes. Strain the liquid into a pan and, if necessary, reduce until only ⅔ cup remains. Add the beef stock.

Preheat the oven to 400°F. Heat half the oil in a flameproof casserole and fry the sausages over high heat to brown all over. Remove with a slotted spoon and set aside. Add the remaining oil and fry the onion, garlic and sage for 5 minutes. Stir in the cabbage and continue to fry for 5 minutes longer. Combine the tomatoes, tomato paste, chili sauce and stock. Pour into the casserole and add the lentils and sausages.

Combine the topping ingredients and scatter over the casserole. Drizzle over a little oil. Cover and bake for 20 minutes. Remove the lid and bake for 20 minutes longer until the topping is golden.   SERVES 4

TOP: *Lamb Steaks with Beans*

BOTTOM: *Sausages Baked with Cabbage and Lentils*

Stuffed Pork Tenderloin

2 x 1-pound PIECES PORK TENDERLOIN
¹/₂ quantity PARSLEY PESTO (SEE PAGE 20)
1 LEMON, THINLY SLICED
16 cloves GARLIC
16 FRESH BAY LEAVES
3 tablespoons OLIVE OIL
1 tablespoon BUTTER
3 GREEN DESSERT APPLES
1 tablespoon BROWN SUGAR
1 tablespoon BALSAMIC VINEGAR

Preheat the oven to 375°F. Rinse and dry the pork. Use a sharp knife to cut along the length of each tenderloin, without cutting in half. Open out each and smother with the parsley pesto. Cut the lemon slices in half and arrange them in the center of the pork with the garlic cloves. Tie the tenderloin back together with string at 1-inch intervals. Tuck bay leaves under some of the string as you go. Cover and marinate overnight.

Heat 2 tablespoons oil in a nonstick skillet. Add the tenderloins and brown all over. Transfer to a roasting pan and roast for 40-45 minutes. Meanwhile, heat the remaining oil with the butter in the skillet. Quarter, core and thickly slice the apples and fry for 2-3 minutes on each side until golden. Remove with a slotted spoon. Stir the sugar and vinegar into the pan, then add to the apples and set aside.

Remove the pork from the pan, cover with foil and let it stand for 5 minutes while finishing the sauce. Scrape all the pork juices into a pan and add the apples and their juices. Bring to a boil, then simmer for 2-3 minutes until thick. Serve the pork in thick slices with the apple sauce.

SERVES 4

RIGHT: Stuffed Pork Tenderloin

Beef with Raisins and Pine Nuts

2 pounds BRAISING STEAK, CUBED

2 tablespoons SEASONED FLOUR

6 tablespoons OLIVE OIL

2/3 cup BEER

1 LARGE ONION, CHOPPED

1 clove GARLIC, CHOPPED

1 tablespoon CHOPPED FRESH THYME

1 tablespoon CHOPPED FRESH ROSEMARY NEEDLES

2 teaspoons PAPRIKA

1 teaspoon GROUND CINNAMON

1 x 14 1/2-ounce CAN CRUSHED TOMATOES

2 BAY LEAVES

1 1/4 cups BEEF STOCK

8 ounces BUTTON MUSHROOMS, HALVED IF LARGE

1 RED BELL PEPPER, SEEDED AND DICED

1/3 cup PINE NUTS

1/3 cup RAISINS

Preheat the oven to 350°F. Dust the meat lightly in the flour. Heat half the oil in a nonstick skillet over high heat and fry the meat for 4-5 minutes until well browned. Use a slotted spoon to transfer the beef to a flameproof casserole. Pour the beer into the skillet and scrape all the meat juices and bits away from the bottom. Pour into the casserole and dry the pan. Heat 1 tablespoon oil and fry the onion, garlic and herbs for 5 minutes. Stir in the spices and cook for 5 minutes. Transfer to the casserole and add the tomatoes, bay leaves and stock. Bring to a boil, then cover and bake for 2 1/2 hours.

Heat the remaining oil in the skillet and fry the mushrooms and pepper for 5 minutes until soft. Add to the casserole with the pine nuts and raisins. Bake for 30 minutes longer.   SERVES 4

Marinated Pork with Potatoes

2 pounds LEAN BONELESS PORK, CUBED

4 tablespoons OLIVE OIL

1 pound SMALL POTATOES, HALVED

8 ounces PEARL ONIONS

1 head FENNEL, CHOPPED

1 1/4 cups CHICKEN STOCK

Marinade

2 tablespoons EXTRA-VIRGIN OLIVE OIL

6 tablespoons DRY WHITE WINE

1/2 ONION, DICED

2 tablespoons CHOPPED FRESH PARSLEY

1 DRIED RED CHILI, SEEDED AND CRUSHED

2 teaspoons PAPRIKA

Place the pork in a shallow, nonmetallic dish. Combine the marinade ingredients, pour over the pork, cover and leave to marinate overnight.

Preheat the oven to 375°F. Remove pork from marinade and pat dry. Strain the liquid from the marinade. Reserve. Heat 2 tablespoons oil in a nonstick skillet and fry the pork over high heat for 5-6 minutes until well browned. Transfer to a flameproof casserole. Add the remaining oil to the skillet and fry the potatoes, onions and fennel for 10 minutes until golden. Add the reserved marinade and transfer to the casserole. Add the stock and, bring to a boil, then cover and bake for 1 1/2 hours until the pork is tender.   SERVES 4

RIGHT: Beef with Raisins and Pine Nuts

Vegetable Dishes

This selection of classic food from southern Europe includes Imam Biyaldi, a Turkish eggplant dish. Its name means "the high priest swooned." Legend tells us that when the priest first tasted it he either swooned with delight, or fainted when he heard how much olive oil it contained, and its cost.

Fritto Misto with Lemon and Thyme Mayonnaise

2 pounds MIXED VEGETABLES (CARROTS, ZUCCHINI, ASPARAGUS TIPS, GREEN BEANS, BELL PEPPERS, FENNEL, POTATOES, BROCCOLI FLOWERETS, CAULIFLOWER FLOWERETS AND SO ON)

VEGETABLE OIL FOR DEEP-FRYING

Lemon and Thyme Mayonnaise

1/2 quantity MAYONNAISE (SEE PAGE 18)

1 tablespoon CHOPPED FRESH THYME

1 tablespoon LEMON JUICE

1 teaspoon GRATED LEMON PEEL

Batter

2 EGGS, SEPARATED

2 tablespoons OLIVE OIL

1 cup BEER

1 1/4 cups ALL-PURPOSE FLOUR

1/2 teaspoon SALT

2 tablespoons CHOPPED FRESH BASIL

Trim and peel the vegetables as necessary, then cut into thin slices or bite-size pieces. Make the mayonnaise according to the recipe on page 18, adding the chopped thyme and lemon juice and peel with the egg yolks. Cover and set aside.

Put about 4 inches oil into a deep, heavy-based saucepan and heat to 350°F: use a candy thermometer or test if a cube of bread browns in 30 seconds. Meanwhile, beat all the batter ingredients, except the egg whites, together until smooth. Beat the egg whites until stiff, but not dry, then carefully fold into the batter until evenly combined.

Dip the vegetables in the batter in batches. Shake off the excess and fry for 2-3 minutes until the coating is crisp and golden. Drain on paper towels and keep warm. Repeat with the remaining vegetables and serve immediately with the lemon and thyme mayonnaise.

SERVES 6-8

RIGHT: Fritto Misto with Lemon and Thyme Mayonnaise

Stuffed Artichokes

6 LARGE GLOBE ARTICHOKES
1 LEMON, HALVED
2/3 cup OLIVE OIL
juice of 1 LEMON
2/3 cup DRY WHITE WINE
2 cloves GARLIC, CHOPPED
1 sprig EACH FRESH PARSLEY, THYME
AND ROSEMARY
2 cloves GARLIC, CRUSHED
grated peel of 1 LEMON
2 tablespoons CHOPPED FRESH BASIL
1 tablespoon CHOPPED FRESH THYME
1 x 4-ounce piece PROSCIUTTO, DICED
1/2 cup CHOPPED, DRAINED SUN-DRIED
TOMATOES IN OIL
2 tablespoons PINE NUTS
1/3 cup FRESHLY GRATED PARMESAN CHEESE

Preheat the oven to 400°F. Snap off the artichoke stems fairly close to the base and cut 1 inch off the top of the bulb. Pull away the tough outer leaves around the base and cut each bulb in half lengthwise. Scoop out the spiky choke in the center and discard. Rub the artichokes all over with the halved lemon. Reserve 2 tablespoons of oil and mix the rest with the lemon juice, wine, garlic and herbs. Lightly season. Pour into a large flameproof casserole and add the artichokes, cut sides down. Bring to a boil, cover and simmer for 45 minutes until tender.

Mix all the remaining ingredients, except the cheese, together. Turn up the artichokes, spoon in the mixture, scatter the cheese over and bake for 30 minutes until golden and bubbling.   SERVES 6

Fennel and Borlotti Bean Bake

2/3 cup DRIED BORLOTTI BEANS,
SOAKED OVERNIGHT, DRAINED
4 SMALL HEADS FENNEL, TRIMMED
6 tablespoons OLIVE OIL
1 ONION, THINLY SLICED
2 cloves GARLIC, CHOPPED
1 tablespoon EACH CHOPPED FRESH ROSEMARY NEEDLES
AND THYME
2/3 cup DRY WHITE WINE
1 1/2 pounds RIPE TOMATOES, PEELED, SEEDED
AND CHOPPED
2-ounce CAN ANCHOVIES IN OIL, DRAINED AND
CHOPPED
1/3 cup CHOPPED PITTED GREEN OLIVES
2 tablespoons CAPERS, DRAINED
1 pound POTATOES, COOKED AND THINLY
SLICED
1/3 cup GRATED GRUYÈRE CHEESE

Put the beans in a pan with 5 cups cold water. Boil rapidly for 10 minutes. Cover. Simmer for 40 minutes. Drain, rinse under cold water and drain again.

Preheat the oven to 400°F. Cut the fennel into thin slices. Heat the oil in a large skillet and fry the fennel for 6-8 minutes until golden. Remove from the pan. Set aside. Fry the onion, garlic and herbs in the pan for 5 minutes. Add the wine and boil rapidly for 5 minutes. Stir in the tomatoes and return the fennel. Cover and simmer for 15 minutes. Season. Stir in the remaining ingredients, except the potatoes and cheese. Add the beans and transfer to a deep baking dish. Top with the potato slices and sprinkle with cheese. Bake for 30 minutes.   SERVES 6

RIGHT: Stuffed Artichokes

Chick-peas with Spinach, Raisins and Pine Nuts

6 tablespoons OLIVE OIL

1 SMALL ONION, SLICED

1 clove GARLIC, CHOPPED

3 cups PEELED AND CUBED POTATOES

2 teaspoons CUMIN SEEDS, LIGHTLY CRUSHED

2 teaspoons PAPRIKA

1 teaspoon CHILI POWDER

1 x 14-ounce CAN CHICK-PEAS

2/3 cup VEGETABLE STOCK

1 pound FRESH SPINACH LEAVES

1/3 cup RAISINS

pinch GRATED NUTMEG

juice of 1/2 LEMON

2 1/2 tablespoons PINE NUTS, TOASTED

EXTRA-VIRGIN OLIVE OIL, TO DRIZZLE

Heat 4 tablespoons of the oil in a nonstick skillet and fry the onion and garlic for 5 minutes until softened. Add the potatoes and spices and fry for 10 minutes until golden. Add the chick-peas, their liquid and the vegetable stock. Cover and simmer for 10 minutes until the potatoes are cooked.

Meanwhile, trim and wash the spinach and roughly shred. Heat the remaining oil in a large pan. Stir-fry the spinach for 3 to 4 minutes until just wilted. Stir into the potatoes, with the raisins and cook for 2 minutes. Season with the nutmeg, some salt and pepper and squeeze a little lemon juice over. Top with the pine nuts, drizzle some extra oil over, if wished, and serve.   SERVES 6-8

Imam Biyaldi

4 SMALL EGGPLANTS (ABOUT 6 INCHES LONG)

1/2 cup OLIVE OIL

1 SMALL ONION, SLICED

1 RED PEPPER, SEEDED AND THINLY SLICED

1 clove GARLIC, CHOPPED

1 tablespoon CHOPPED FRESH CILANTRO

2 teaspoons GROUND CORIANDER

2 teaspoons PAPRIKA

1 teaspoon CUMIN SEEDS

1 teaspoon GROUND CINNAMON

2 LARGE TOMATOES, PEELED AND CHOPPED

2 tablespoons CHOPPED, DRAINED SUN-DRIED TOMATOES IN OIL

1 tablespoon LEMON JUICE

1 cup VEGETABLE STOCK, BOILING

PLAIN YOGURT, CHOPPED FRESH CILANTRO AND TOASTED CASHEW NUTS, TO GARNISH

Preheat the oven to 400°F. Wash and dry the eggplants. Cut a long deep slit in each one without cutting in half. Heat the oil in a deep, nonstick skillet. Add the eggplants and fry for 6-8 minutes until browned all over. Transfer to a baking dish. Fry the onion, pepper, garlic, fresh cilantro and spices in the skillet for 5 minutes. Add the tomatoes, sun-dried tomatoes and lemon juice and cook gently for 15 minutes.

Carefully pull open the slit in each eggplant and spoon in the tomato sauce. Spoon the remaining sauce around the eggplants. Pour in the boiling stock. Cover and bake for 30 minutes. Remove the lid and continue to bake for 20 minutes longer. Garnish with a little yogurt, cilantro and cashew nuts. Serve at room temperature.   SERVES 4

TOP: *Chick-peas with Spinach, Raisins and Pine Nuts*

BOTTOM: *Imam Biyaldi*

Baked Red Bell Peppers Topped with Mozzarella

3 LARGE RED BELL PEPPERS
3 PLUM TOMATOES, PEELED AND HALVED
4 tablespoons OLIVE OIL
1 tablespoon BALSAMIC VINEGAR
2 cloves GARLIC, CRUSHED
2 tablespoons CHOPPED FRESH BASIL
2 teaspoons GRATED LEMON PEEL
12 ANCHOVY FILLETS IN OIL, DRAINED
6 ounces BUFFALO MOZZARELLA CHEESE,
SLICED INTO 6 SLICES

Preheat the oven to 400°F. Cut the peppers in half lengthwise through the stems, remove the seeds and place, cut sides up, in a roasting pan. Place a tomato half in each one. Mix the oil, vinegar, garlic, basil and lemon peel together. Season to taste. Divide between each pepper and bake for 40 minutes. Place 2 anchovy fillets and a slice of mozzarella on each pepper. Return to the oven for 15-20 minutes longer. Serve immediately.

SERVES 6

Mashed Potato with Thyme Oil

2 pounds FLOURY POTATOES, CUBED
1/2 quantity THYME OIL (SEE PAGE 16)
2 tablespoons MILK
2 tablespoons FRESHLY GRATED PARMESAN CHEESE

Boil the potatoes in a large pan of lightly salted water for 12-15 minutes. Drain and return to the pan. Heat gently for a few seconds to dry the potatoes out. Mash the potatoes, gradually adding the oil and milk to form a soft mixture. Stir in the cheese and season. SERVES 4

Navy Beans with Oil, Lemon and Anchovies

1 1/3 cups DRIED NAVY BEANS, SOAKED
OVERNIGHT
1 BOUQUET GARNI
6 tablespoons EXTRA-VIRGIN OLIVE OIL
2 cloves GARLIC, CHOPPED
grated peel and juice of 1 LEMON
8 ANCHOVY FILLETS, DRAINED AND CHOPPED
4 tablespoons CHOPPED FRESH PARSLEY
pinch SUGAR

Drain the beans and place in a large pan with 5 cups cold water and the bouquet garni. Boil rapidly for 10 minutes. Lower the heat, cover and simmer for 30 minutes or until tender. Meanwhile, heat 2 tablespoons of the oil in a small skillet. Add the chopped garlic and fry gently for 4-5 minutes until softened and golden. Mash the garlic with a fork. Cool. Beat in the remaining ingredients and season to taste. Drain the beans, toss with the olive oil mixture and leave to cool at room temperature. SERVES 4

TOP: Baked Red Bell Peppers Topped with Mozzarella
BOTTOM: Navy Beans with Oil, Lemon and Anchovies

Salads

It is perhaps with salads, or more specifically salad dressings, that olive oil is most closely associated. Recipes for five dressings can be found on page 13. The following dishes offer more unusual ideas for using olive oil with both raw and cooked ingredients.

Marinated Goat Cheese Salad

6 thick slices CIABATTA BREAD OR FRENCH BREAD

Marinated Cheese
6 cloves GARLIC
at least 4 tablespoons EXTRA-VIRGIN OLIVE OIL, PLUS EXTRA TO COVER
8 ounces FIRM GOAT CHEESE, RIND REMOVED
4 FRESH RED OR GREEN CHILIES
1 tablespoon CUMIN SEEDS, TOASTED
4 BAY LEAVES, BRUISED
2 sprigs FRESH ROSEMARY
1 teaspoon WHITE PEPPERCORNS

Warm Oil Dressing
2 tablespoons CAPERS IN BRINE, DRAINED
1 tablespoon CHOPPED FRESH BASIL
4 SUN-DRIED TOMATOES IN OIL, DRAINED AND SLICED
1 tablespoon BALSAMIC VINEGAR

4 ounces MIXED SALAD LEAVES
2 tablespoons PINE NUTS, TOASTED

To make the marinated cheese, place the garlic in a small pan and add enough oil to just cover. Heat gently for 10 minutes until the cloves are tender and golden. Remove from the heat and leave to cool. Divide the cheese into six pieces and roll each piece into a small ball. Arrange the cheeses in a clean jar, layering them with all the remaining marinade ingredients, including the cooked garlic. Pour in enough oil to completely cover the cheese and seal well. Store in a cool place for at least three days but no more than one week.

Preheat the oven to 400°F. Carefully remove the cheese and garlic cloves from the oil and drain on paper towels. Reserve 6 tablespoons oil from the jar. Place the bread slices in the oven for 15 minutes, turning once, until crisp and golden. Remove and immediately spread the garlic cloves on the bread. Cool. Heat half the reserved oil in a small pan, add the capers, basil and tomatoes and heat until almost boiling. Beat in the remaining oil and the vinegar.

Rinse and dry the salad leaves and arrange on plates. Spread one cheese ball over each garlic toast and place in the middle of each salad. Scatter the pine nuts over and immediately drizzle the warm olive oil dressing over. Serve immediately.　　　　SERVES 6

RIGHT: Marinated Goat Cheese Salad

Broiled Tomato and Asparagus Salad

12 THICK ASPARAGUS SPEARS, TRIMMED
EXTRA-VIRGIN OLIVE OIL
8 RIPE PLUM TOMATOES, PEELED,
QUARTERED AND SEEDED
2 ounces BABY SPINACH LEAVES
6 ounces BUFFALO MOZZARELLA CHEESE, SLICED
1/4 cup RIPE OLIVES
4 tablespoons PESTO (SEE PAGE 20)

Slice the asparagus in half and brush with a little oil. Broil for 6-8 minutes, turning frequently, until charred and tender. Drizzle a little oil over the tomato quarters and broil for 2-3 minutes until just softened. Leave both to cool. Arrange the asparagus and tomatoes on plates. Add the spinach leaves, mozzarella and olives. Mix the pesto with oil to make a dressing and drizzle over the salad. Serve immediately.   SERVES 4

Seeded Yam Salad

Serve this yam salad at room temperature.

2 pounds YAMS, PEELED
6 tablespoons EXTRA-VIRGIN OLIVE OIL
SALT AND PEPPER
1 tablespoon EACH SUNFLOWER SEEDS, PUMPKIN SEEDS,
SESAME SEEDS AND POPPY SEEDS
1 tablespoon BALSAMIC VINEGAR
2 tablespoons CHOPPED FRESH CILANTRO

Preheat the oven to 425°F. Rinse and dry the yams and cut into large cubes. Place in a roasting pan to fit in a single layer. Add 2 tablespoons of oil. Season lightly, toss well and roast for 25 minutes, stirring occasionally, until golden and tender. Transfer to a large bowl. Heat the remaining oil in a pan. Stir-fry the seeds until lightly golden. Remove from the heat. Set aside to cool. Beat in the vinegar and cilantro, pour over the potatoes and toss well.   SERVES 4

Smoked Chicken and Avocado Salad

1/2 quantity MAYONNAISE (SEE PAGE 18)
1 tablespoon CHOPPED FRESH TARRAGON
1 pound BONED, SKINLESS SMOKED CHICKEN BREAST
4 RIPE PLUM TOMATOES
1 AVOCADO
2 tablespoons EXTRA-VIRGIN OLIVE OIL
TARRAGON SPRIGS, TO GARNISH

Make up a half quantity of mayonnaise according to the recipe on page 18. Stir in the tarragon. Cover and set aside for 30 minutes. Roughly shred the chicken and stir in the mayonnaise. Thinly slice the tomatoes and arrange on 4 plates. Peel, halve and seed the avocado and thinly slice. Arrange over the tomato slices, drizzle the oil over and season. Heap the chicken into the middle of each plate. Garnish with a sprig of tarragon.   SERVES 4

TOP: Broiled Tomato and Asparagus Salad, Seeded Yam Salad
BOTTOM: Smoked Chicken and Avocado Salad

Bitter Salad with Caesar Dressing

❧

1 head BELGIAN ENDIVE
1/2 head RADICCHIO
1 ounce FRISÉE LETTUCE LEAVES
1 ounce ARUGULA LEAVES
1 ounce ESCAROLE LETTUCE LEAVES
2 tablespoons OLIVE OIL
2 cloves GARLIC, ROUGHLY CHOPPED
4 thick slices BREAD, CRUSTS REMOVED AND CUBED
SLIVERS OF PARMESAN CHEESE, TO SERVE

Dressing
1 EGG YOLK
1 tablespoon LEMON JUICE
1 clove GARLIC, CRUSHED
2 ANCHOVY FILLETS, DRAINED AND CHOPPED
pinch SUGAR
2 teaspoons WORCESTERSHIRE SAUCE
dash HOT-PEPPER SAUCE
1/2 cup EXTRA-VIRGIN OLIVE OIL

Tear all the salad leaves into bite-sized pieces. Rinse, drain well and pat dry. Transfer to a plastic bag, seal and chill for 30 minutes. Heat the oil in a skillet and fry the garlic over low heat until golden. Strain the oil into a clean pan and add the bread. Stir-fry for 2-3 minutes until crisp and golden. Drain the croutons on paper towels. Beat all the dressing ingredients together except the oil. Then gradually beat in the oil, a little at a time, until the dressing is thick and glossy. Season to taste and set aside.

Return the salad leaves to room temperature. Place in a large bowl and scatter the croutons over. Drizzle the dressing over, top with the slivers of Parmesan and serve immediately. SERVES 4

Marinated Scallops with East-West Dressing

❧

1 ounce FERMENTED BLACK BEANS IN JAR
12 LARGE SCALLOPS
4 SUN-DRIED TOMATOES IN OIL, DRAINED AND CHOPPED
2-4 tablespoons EXTRA-VIRGIN OLIVE OIL
4 ounces MIXED SALAD LEAVES, RINSED AND DRIED

Marinade
2 tablespoons SHERRY
2 tablespoons OLIVE OIL
1 tablespoon SOY SAUCE
1 teaspoon GRATED FRESH GINGER ROOT
1 FRESH RED CHILI, SEEDED AND CHOPPED
grated rind and juice of 1/2 ORANGE

Rinse the beans and soak in cold water for 1 hour. Drain, rinse again and pat dry. Discard tough membrane from each scallop. Separate the corals and slice the flesh in half, rinse and pat dry. Place the scallops and corals in a shallow nonmetallic dish. Combine the marinade ingredients and pour over, cover and marinate 1 hour.

Strain the marinade juices into a small pan. Add soaked beans and bring to a boil. Set aside. Purée tomatoes and 2 tablespoons of the oil. Beat into the marinade. Heat the remaining oil in a skillet. Dry scallops. Sear over high heat for 1 minute on each side. Spoon onto the salad, pour dressing over and serve.

SERVES 4

RIGHT: Marinated Scallops with East-West Dressing

Broiled Vegetable Salad with Skordalià

2 YELLOW OR RED BELL PEPPERS, SEEDED
AND QUARTERED

1½ *cups* SCRUBBED AND THINLY SLICED RAW BEETS

1¼ *cups* JERUSALEM ARTICHOKES, SCRUBBED AND
THINLY SLICED

1 EGGPLANT, THINLY SLICED

2 *small* ZUCCHINI, SLICED LENGTHWISE

1 *small head* RADICCHIO, CUT INTO THIN WEDGES

1 *head* FENNEL, THINLY SLICED LENGTHWISE

8 *ounces* ASPARAGUS SPEARS, TRIMMED

¼ *cup* LEMON CITRUS OIL (SEE PAGE 16)

1 *quantity* SKORDALIÀ (SEE PAGE 18)

Brush all the vegetables with citrus oil and broil each vegetable separately until charred and tender. (The cooking times will vary depending on the vegetable.) Arrange on a large platter and drizzle any remaining oil over. Serve at room temperature with skordalià.

SERVES 4-6

Italian Bean and Seafood Salad

This recipe combines two classic Italian dishes into one to make a delicious and substantial salad.

20 FRESH MUSSELS, SCRUBBED

⅔ *cup* FISH OR VEGETABLE STOCK

1 *pound* SMALL RAW SHRIMP, SHELLED

8 BABY SQUID, GUTTED, RINSED AND SLICED

1 *tablespoon* OLIVE OIL

8 *ounces* FRESH TUNA FISH, CUBED

1 RED ONION, THINLY SLICED

2 *cloves* GARLIC, CHOPPED

2 *stalks* CELERY, THINLY SLICED

8 SUN-DRIED TOMATOES IN OIL,
DRAINED AND SLICED

1 x 14 ½-*ounce* CAN CANNELLINI BEANS, DRAINED

⅓ *cup* RIPE OLIVES

Dressing

6 *tablespoons* EXTRA-VIRGIN OLIVE OIL

1 *tablespoon* BALSAMIC VINEGAR

2 *tablespoons* CHOPPED FRESH BASIL

1 *tablespoon* CHOPPED FRESH ROSEMARY NEEDLES

Rinse the mussels for several minutes under cold water. Discard any that do not close when tapped. Place in a saucepan with the stock. Bring to a boil, then cover and simmer for 5 minutes until all the shells have opened. Discard any that remain closed. Strain the liquid into a clean pan. Set the mussels aside to cool. Add the shrimp and squid to the poaching liquid. Bring to a boil, then simmer for 30 seconds and set aside to cool in the liquid. Heat the oil in a pan and gently fry the tuna for 3 minutes. Remove from the heat. Cool.

Combine all the remaining ingredients in a large bowl. Shell the mussels if wished. Remove the shrimp and squid from their cooking liquid and add to the salad with the tuna. Strain 4 tablespoons of the poaching liquid into a bowl. Beat in the dressing ingredients. Season to taste. Pour over the salad, toss well and chill for 1 hour. Serve at room temperature. SERVES 4

TOP: Broiled Vegetable Salad with Skordalià

BOTTOM: Italian Bean and Seafood Salad

Rice and Pasta

The rice dishes in this chapter may appear to be similar in style at first, but you will find they are totally different in taste. Pasta and olive oil are natural partners. Most of the following pasta recipes are served with simple, olive oil-based sauces.

Rice with Seafood and Aïoli

This dish is unusual in that the seafood is served at room temperature either with the hot rice or as a separate course.

1 pound FRESH MUSSELS
1 pound SMALL SQUID, DRESSED
12 RAW JUMBO SHRIMP OR TIGER PRAWNS
4¹/2 cups FISH STOCK
pinch SAFFRON STRANDS
6 tablespoons OLIVE OIL
1 ONION, FINELY CHOPPED
4 cloves GARLIC, CHOPPED
2 teaspoons CRUSHED CHILI
1¹/2 cups ARBORIO RICE
2/3 cup DRY WHITE WINE
4 RIPE TOMATOES, PEELED, SEEDED AND DICED
1/2 quantity AÏOLI (SEE PAGE 18)

Scrub the mussels and rinse them well. Disgard any that remain open when you tap them. Place in a large pan with only the water on the shells. Cover and cook over medium heat for 5 minutes until the shells open.

Strain the liquid into a pan and reserve the mussels. Discard any that remain closed. Slice the squid. Poach the squid rings in the mussel liquid for 2-3 minutes until opaque, then remove and set aside. Poach the shrimp in the same liquid for 5 minutes, then remove from the pan and set aside. Strain the liquid and make up to 5 cups with the fish stock. Add the saffron strands. Cover and set all the seafood aside.

Heat the oil in a large skillet. Add the onion, garlic and chili and fry for 10 minutes, stirring occasionally, until browned. Add the rice and stir-fry for 1 minute, then pour in the wine. Boil rapidly for 5 minutes. Stir in the tomatoes and stock and cook for 25 minutes or until the rice is tender. (There should still be some stock which has not been absorbed.)

Spoon the hot rice into a dish. Serve the seafood at room temperature with the aïoli. SERVES 4-6

RIGHT: Rice with Seafood and Aïoli

Pasta with Broccoli and Walnuts

❦

1 1/2 pounds BROCCOLI
SALT AND PEPPER
12 ounces DRIED PASTA
4 tablespoons EXTRA-VIRGIN OLIVE OIL
1 clove GARLIC, CHOPPED
1 RED CHILI, SEEDED AND CHOPPED
4 tablespoons WALNUT PASTE (SEE PAGE 22)
GRATED PECORINO CHEESE OR SLIVERS
OF PARMESAN CHEESE, TO SERVE

Trim the broccoli, cut into bite-sized flowerets and slice the stems. Bring a large pan of lightly salted water to a rolling boil. Add the pasta, return to a boil and simmer for 10-12 minutes until the pasta is *al dente*. Meanwhile, heat the oil in a large skillet, then fry the broccoli, garlic and chili for 5-6 minutes until the broccoli is tender. Drain the pasta and toss with the walnut paste. Stir into the broccoli mixture. Serve with the cheese. SERVES 4

Homemade Tagliatelle with Garlic and Chili

❦

A pasta machine is required to make fresh tagliatelle. Investing in one, although fairly expensive, is money well spent, as homemade pasta cannot be bettered.

2 cups ALL-PURPOSE FLOUR
1 teaspoon SALT
2 EGGS
1 EGG YOLK
1 tablespoon EXTRA-VIRGIN OLIVE OIL

Sauce
6 tablespoons CARAMELIZED GARLIC OIL (SEE PAGE 14)
2 cloves GARLIC, SLICED
2 RED CHILIES, SEEDED AND CHOPPED
grated peel of 1 LEMON
4 tablespoons CHOPPED FRESH BASIL
FRESHLY GRATED PARMESAN CHEESE,
TO SERVE

Start by making the pasta. Sift the flour and salt into a large bowl, make a well in the middle and gradually work in the eggs, egg yolk, oil and 1-2 tablespoons water to form a soft dough. Knead for 4-5 minutes until the dough is smooth. Cover and set aside for 30 minutes.

Divide the dough into 8 pieces and shape into small, flat rectangles. Pass each piece twice through the widest setting of the pasta machine, then turn to the next setting, repeat twice and then again at each setting to form very thin sheets of pasta. Cut each sheet in half crosswise and hang over a wooden pole for 5 minutes. Pass each sheet through the tagliatelle cutter on the machine and hang the noodles over the pole for 5 minutes longer. Curl into nests and leave on a floured dish towel until required.

Bring a large pan of water to a rolling boil. Meanwhile, make the sauce. Heat the oil in a skillet. Add the garlic, chilies and lemon peel and fry for 2-3 minutes until they start to brown. Add 1 teaspoon salt to the water, return to a boil and cook the pasta for 1-2 minutes until *al dente*. Drain. Toss with the garlic oil and stir in the basil. Top with plenty of Parmesan and serve. SERVES 3-4

RIGHT: Homemade Tagliatelle with Garlic and Chili

Spaghetti with Scallops and Oyster Mushrooms

1 pound FRESH BAY SCALLOPS, SHELLED
6 tablespoons EXTRA-VIRGIN OLIVE OIL
2 cloves GARLIC, CRUSHED
12 ounces OYSTER MUSHROOMS
1 pound FRESH SPAGHETTI
SALT AND PEPPER
2 tablespoons CHOPPED FRESH CHERVIL

Marinade
6 tablespoons EXTRA-VIRGIN OLIVE OIL
6 tablespoons DRY WHITE WINE
2 RIPE TOMATOES, PEELED, SEEDED AND DICED
2 tablespoons CHOPPED FRESH CHERVIL
4 sprigs FRESH THYME, BRUISED
1 teaspoon CORIANDER SEEDS, BRUISED

Rinse and dry the scallops and cut away the tough gray membranes. Place in a shallow nonmetallic dish. Combine the marinade ingredients together, pour over the scallops, cover and leave to marinate overnight.

Carefully remove the scallops from their marinade and pat dry with paper towels. Heat 2 tablespoons of the oil in a large skillet. Add the garlic and fry for 1 minute, stir in the mushrooms and fry for 3-4 minutes longer until golden. Cook the spaghetti in a large pan of boiling, salted water for 3-4 minutes until *al dente*. Meanwhile, heat 1 tablespoon oil in a heavy-based skillet and sear the scallops for 1 minute on each side until browned. Add to the mushrooms with the chervil, then remove pan from the heat. Drain the spaghetti and toss immediately with the sauce and the remaining oil. Season and serve immediately.   SERVES 4

Penne with New Potatoes, Asparagus and Tapenade

1 pound NEW POTATOES, SCRUBBED
SALT
1 pound ASPARAGUS SPEARS
12 ounces DRIED PENNE
2 tablespoons EXTRA-VIRGIN OLIVE OIL
4 tablespoons TAPENADE (SEE PAGE 22)

Cook the potatoes in boiling salted water for 10-12 minutes until just tender. Drain, rinse under cold water and pat dry. Trim and roughly chop the asparagus and blanch in boiling salted water for 2 minutes. Drain, refresh under cold water and pat dry.

Bring a large pan of lightly salted, boiling water to a rolling boil. Add the penne, return to a boil and cook for 10-12 minutes until *al dente*. Meanwhile, heat the oil in a large skillet. Add the potatoes and stir-fry for 2-3 minutes until they start to brown. Add the asparagus and stir-fry for 1 minute longer. Stir in the tapenade and keep warm. Drain the pasta, toss with the tapenade mixture and serve immediately.   SERVES 4

TOP: Spaghetti with Scallops and Oyster Mushrooms
BOTTOM: Penne with New Potatoes, Asparagus and Tapenade

Jambalaya

2 teaspoons CELERY SALT

1 teaspoon PAPRIKA

1/2 teaspoon MUSTARD POWDER

1/4 teaspoon GROUND CLOVES

pinch GROUND CARDAMOM

4 tablespoons OLIVE OIL

1 pound CHICKEN PIECES, SKINNED

pinch SUGAR

1 ONION, CHOPPED

2 stalks CELERY, CHOPPED

2 cloves GARLIC, CRUSHED

1 tablespoon CHOPPED FRESH THYME

1 RED BELL PEPPER, SEEDED AND FINELY CHOPPED

1 x 14-ounce CAN CRUSHED TOMATOES

1/2 cup WILD RICE

2 1/2 cups VEGETABLE STOCK

1 cup LONG-GRAIN RICE

1 1/2 cups DICED COOKED HAM

1 pound RAW JUMBO SHRIMP

8 ounces CLAMS

Combine the first 5 ingredients in a bowl to make a seasoning. Set aside. Heat the oil in a large skillet or flameproof casserole, then fry the chicken pieces for 5-6 minutes until evenly browned. Remove with a slotted spoon. Add a pinch of salt and sugar, the onion, celery, garlic, thyme, red bell pepper and seasoning mix. Fry for 10 minutes until golden. Add the tomatoes, wild rice and stock. Return the chicken to the pan, bring to a boil, cover and simmer for 20 minutes. Add the long-grain rice, stir well, cover and cook for 20 minutes. Stir in the ham, shrimp and clams and continue to cook, covered, for 15 minutes longer until both rices are tender and the shrimp are pink and clams are open. Season to taste and serve immediately. SERVES 6-8

Chorizo and Radicchio Risotto

12 ounces CHORIZO OR OTHER SPICY SAUSAGE, CHOPPED

4 tablespoons OLIVE OIL

2 RED ONIONS, CHOPPED

4 cloves GARLIC, CRUSHED

1 teaspoon CRUSHED CHILI

1 tablespoon CHOPPED FRESH SAGE

1 3/4 cups ARBORIO RICE

2/3 cup FRUITY RED WINE

3 3/4 cups CHICKEN STOCK

4 cups SHREDDED RADICCHIO

1/3 cup RIPE OLIVES

1/4 cup MASCARPONE CHEESE

FRESHLY GRATED PARMESAN CHEESE

Dry-fry the chorizo in a large, heavy-based skillet for 4-5 minutes until golden and the fat is released. Use a slotted spoon to remove from the pan; set aside. Add the oil to the pan and fry the onions, garlic and chili for 15 minutes until golden. Add the sage and rice and stir-fry for 1 minute. Pour in the wine. Boil rapidly for 3 minutes. Return the sausage to the pan and gradually add the stock 2/3 cup at a time. Cook for 25-30 minutes until the rice is tender. Add the radicchio with the final addition of stock. Stir in the olives and mascarpone cheese. Season to taste. Serve with Parmesan. SERVES 6

RIGHT: Chorizo and Radicchio Risotto

Pizzas, Breads, Cakes & Cookies

Using olive oil for baking sweet things is a familiar feature of Mediterranean cooking.
It is best to use plain olive oil rather than extra-virgin for these. It is an integral ingredient
in the following pizza and bread recipes, giving them a subtle fragrance.

Basic Pizza Base

2 cups BREAD FLOUR, PLUS EXTRA FOR DUSTING
1/2 teaspoon SALT
1/2 teaspoon RAPID-RISE ACTIVE DRY YEAST
2/3 cup WARM WATER
1 tablespoon EXTRA-VIRGIN OLIVE OIL

Sift the flour and salt into a bowl and stir in the yeast. Make a well in the middle and gradually work in the warm water and oil to form a soft dough. Knead on a lightly floured surface for 8-10 minutes until the dough is smooth and elastic. Place in an oiled bowl, cover with oiled plastic wrap and leave to rise in a warm place for 40 minutes or until double in size.

Preheat the oven to 450°F and place a large baking sheet on the top shelf. Knead the dough lightly for 1 minute. Divide in half. Roll out each half and put each base into a 9-inch pizza plate or shallow cake pan. Spread each base with a topping of your choice and bake on the hot baking sheet for 20 minutes until bubbling and golden. SERVES 2-4

Pesto and Cheese Pizza

1 quantity BASIC PIZZA BASE (SEE ABOVE)
1 quantity PESTO (SEE PAGE 20)
1 1/2 cups FINELY DICED MOZZARELLA CHEESE
8 ounces TALEGGIO OR FONTINA CHEESE, THINLY SLICED
1 tablespoon DRIED OREGANO
EXTRA-VIRGIN OLIVE OIL, TO DRIZZLE
FRESHLY GROUND BLACK PEPPER

Make up the pizza dough and prepare the two bases according to the recipe above. Preheat the oven to 450°F and place a large baking sheet on the top shelf. Spread each pizza base with pesto and top with the two cheeses. Sprinkle the oregano over, drizzle with oil and grind the pepper over. Bake on the hot baking sheet for 20 minutes until bubbling and golden. SERVES 2-4

RIGHT: Pesto and Cheese Pizza

Broiled Tomato and Onion Pizza with Anchovy Paste

1 quantity BASIC PIZZA BASE (SEE PAGE 84)
4 RED ONIONS
2 tablespoons OLIVE OIL
1 pound RIPE PLUM TOMATOES
1/2 quantity ANCHOVY PASTE (SEE PAGE 20)
2 tablespoons CHOPPED FRESH BASIL
1/2 cup FRESHLY GRATED PARMESAN CHEESE
EXTRA-VIRGIN OLIVE OIL, TO DRIZZLE
SALT AND PEPPER

Make up the pizza dough and prepare the bases according to the recipe on page 84. Preheat the oven to 450°F and place a large baking sheet at the top of the oven. Preheat the broiler.

Cut the onions into thin wedges, brush with oil and broil for 15 minutes until golden and tender. Peel, quarter and seed the tomatoes. Place on the broiler pan, drizzle with oil and broil for 5 minutes until softened. Mash with a fork. Spread each pizza base with the anchovy paste and tomato pulp and scatter the broiled onions, basil and cheese over. Drizzle a little more oil over, season, and bake on the hot baking sheet for 20 minutes. SERVES 2-4

Artichoke, Prosciutto and Goat Cheese Pizza

1 quantity BASIC PIZZA BASE (SEE PAGE 84)
one 16-ounce jar ARTICHOKES IN OIL, DRAINED AND SLICED
4 ounces THINLY SLICED PROSCIUTTO, CHOPPED
2 tablespoons CHOPPED FRESH THYME
4 tablespoons DRIED AND PRESERVED CHERRY TOMATOES, DRAINED (SEE PAGE 24)
12 ounces GOAT CHEESE, THINLY SLICED
EXTRA-VIRGIN OLIVE OIL, TO DRIZZLE
SALT AND PEPPER

Make up the pizza dough and prepare the bases according to the recipe on page 84. Preheat the oven to 450°F and place a large baking sheet at the top of the oven. Arrange the artichokes and prosciutto over each base, sprinkle the thyme and tomatoes over and top with the goat cheese. Drizzle extra oil over, season, and bake on the hot baking sheet for 20 minutes until bubbling and golden. SERVES 2-4

TOP: *Broiled Tomato and Onion Pizza with Anchovy Paste*
BOTTOM: *Artichoke, Prosciutto and Goat Cheese Pizza*

Rosemary Focaccia

Italian olive oil bread is best eaten warm. The pan of boiling water in the oven is essential in keeping the bread soft as it bakes.

1/2 ounce COMPRESSED FRESH YEAST
1 cup WARM WATER
4 cups BREAD FLOUR
1/2 teaspoon SUGAR
1 teaspoon SALT
1/4 cup ROSEMARY OIL (SEE PAGE 16)

Topping
2 tablespoons ROSEMARY OIL
2 tablespoons CHOPPED FRESH ROSEMARY NEEDLES
2 teaspoons SEA SALT

Mix the yeast with 1/2 cup of the warm water, 4 tablespoons flour and the sugar until smooth. Cover and leave for 10 minutes until frothy. Sift the remaining flour and salt into a bowl and work in the frothed yeast, another 1/2 cup of the warm water and the oil, to form a soft dough. Knead on a lightly floured surface for 8-10 minutes until smooth and elastic. Place in an oiled bowl, cover with oiled plastic wrap and leave to rise in a warm place for 40 minutes or until double in size.

Roll out the dough to a thin, flat oval about 1/2 inch thick. Place on a greased baking sheet, brush with a little oil, cover and leave to rise for 20 minutes longer. Preheat the oven to 425°F. Place a roasting pan full of hot water on the bottom shelf of the oven. Mix the topping ingredients together. Press thumb indents all over the surface of the dough. Brush the topping over, then bake on the middle shelf for 25 minutes until risen and golden. The base should sound hollow when tapped lightly. Leave to cool slightly on a wire rack and serve warm.

MAKES 1 LARGE LOAF

RIGHT: Rosemary Focaccia

Herb and Cheese Bread

2 tablespoons OLIVE OIL

1/2 ONION, FINELY CHOPPED

1 clove GARLIC, CRUSHED

1 tablespoon CHOPPED FRESH THYME

2 teaspoons DRIED OREGANO

2 teaspoons DRIED MINT

1/2 cup CRUMBLED FETA CHEESE

Dough

1/2 ounce COMPRESSED FRESH YEAST

1 cup plus 2 tablespoons MILK, WARM

2 cups BREAD FLOUR

2 cups WHOLE-WHEAT BREAD FLOUR

pinch SUGAR

1 teaspoon SALT

4 tablespoons EXTRA-VIRGIN OLIVE OIL

Heat the oil in a skillet and fry the onion, garlic and herbs for 10 minutes. Set aside to cool. Meanwhile, blend the yeast, half the warm milk, 1/2 cup of the flour and the sugar together until smooth. Cover and leave in a warm place for 10 minutes until frothy. Sift the remaining flour and salt into a bowl and work in the frothed yeast, remaining warm milk and olive oil to form a soft dough. Knead for 8-10 minutes until smooth and elastic. Place dough in an oiled bowl, cover with oiled plastic wrap and leave to rise in a warm place for 45 minutes or until double in size.

Knock back the dough on a lightly-floured surface and roll out to a 10- x 14-inch rectangle. Scatter the onion mixture over the dough and top with the cheese. Roll up the dough from one short end, wetting the edges and pressing together to seal. Place seam side down on a greased baking sheet. Cover and leave to rise for 30 minutes longer. Preheat the oven to 425°F. Bake for 35 minutes until golden. The underside should sound hollow when tapped. Cool on a wire rack until cool.

MAKES 1 LOAF

Tomato and Mozzarella Bread

2 LOAVES CIABATTA BREAD OR SMALL FRENCH BREAD

2 cloves GARLIC, HALVED

6 tablespoons EXTRA-VIRGIN OLIVE OIL

1/2 quantity RED PESTO (SEE PAGE 20)

12 ounces MOZZARELLA CHEESE, SLICED

Preheat the oven to 400°F. Slice each loaf crosswise at 1-inch intervals without cutting all the way through. Rub all over and between the slices with garlic. Drizzle the oil over and spread the pesto between the slices. Put a slice of cheese between each slice. Wrap in foil and bake for 15 minutes. Open the packages and bake for 5 minutes longer. Serve hot.

SERVES 6-8

TOP: Herb and Cheese Bread

BOTTOM: Tomato and Mozzarella Bread

Walnut and Olive Oil Cake

1½ cups SELF-RISING FLOUR, SIFTED

½ cup SUPERFINE SUGAR

1 cup WALNUTS, FINELY GROUND

grated peel of ½ LEMON

3 EGGS, SEPARATED

½ cup OLIVE OIL

⅓ cup CHOPPED DRIED FIGS

Syrup

1 LEMON

3½ tablespoons HONEY

1 stick CINNAMON

2 DRIED FIGS, SLICED

1 tablespoon BRANDY

YOGURT, TO SERVE

Preheat the oven to 350°F. Combine the flour, sugar, walnuts and lemon peel in a bowl. Beat the egg yolks and oil together, then stir into the dry ingredients. Beat the egg whites until stiff. Stir one-third into the walnut mixture, then fold in the rest along with the figs. Spoon into a greased and lined 8-inch springform cake pan, leveling the surface. Bake for 70 minutes until risen and firm to the touch.

Meanwhile, peel the lemon and cut the peel into thin strips. Squeeze the juice into a small pan and add the peel, honey, cinnamon stick and figs. Bring to a boil, then simmer gently for 2 minutes. Cool and stir in the brandy. Pour syrup over the cake and leave to cool in the pan. Turn out onto a large plate and serve with yogurt.

MAKES 1 x 8-INCH ROUND CAKE

Carrot and Ginger Cake

2 cups WHOLE-WHEAT SELF-RISING FLOUR

2 teaspoons GROUND GINGER

1 teaspoon APPLE PIE SPICE

½ teaspoon SALT

1 cup SUPERFINE SUGAR

3 EGGS

¾ cup plus 2 tablespoons OLIVE OIL

2 tablespoons SYRUP FROM A JAR OF PRESERVED GINGER

3 cups GRATED AND SQUEEZED DRY CARROTS

1 cup BLANCHED HAZELNUTS, FINELY GROUND

⅓ cup GOLDEN RAISINS

2 tablespoons CHOPPED PRESERVED STEM GINGER

2 tablespoons SLIVERED HAZELNUTS

1 tablespoon SHREDLESS MARMALADE

Preheat the oven to 350°F. Sift the flour, spices and salt into a bowl. Beat the sugar, eggs, oil and ginger syrup together for 1 minute until pale and frothy. Beat into the dry ingredients until well combined. Fold in the carrots, hazelnuts, golden raisins and chopped ginger and spoon into a greased and lined 8-inch square cake pan. Sprinkle the slivered hazelnuts over and bake for 1½ hours or until a skewer inserted in the middle comes out clean. Cool in the pan for 10 minutes, then turn out onto a wire rack and brush with the marmalade. Leave to cool completely.

MAKES 1 x 8-INCH SQUARE CAKE

TOP: Walnut and Olive Oil Cake
BOTTOM: Carrot and Ginger Cake

Amaretti Biscotti

2 EGGS

1 cup CONFECTIONERS' SUGAR

2 cups ALL-PURPOSE FLOUR

1 teaspoon BAKING POWDER

pinch SALT

3 tablespoons OLIVE OIL

1 cup BLANCHED ALMONDS, FINELY GROUND AND TOASTED

2 ounces AMARETTI COOKIES, CRUSHED

grated peel of 1/2 LEMON

1/2 cup WHOLE ALMONDS

Preheat the oven to 350°F. Beat the eggs and confectioners' sugar together for 5 minutes, then beat in the flour, baking powder and salt. Stir in all the remaining ingredients, except the whole almonds, to form a slightly sticky dough. Roll out the dough on a lightly floured surface to form a 3-x 12-inch log. Make a deep trench along the middle of the log and press the almonds into the hollow. Roll the sides up and over to enclose the nuts and place seam-side down on a greased baking sheet. Bake for 15 minutes.

Remove from the oven and increase the temperature to 400°F. Cut the log into 1/2-inch slices. Return to the baking sheet, cut sides down, and bake for 20 minutes longer until golden, turning over half way through. Cool on a wire rack. Store in an airtight container.

MAKES 24 COOKIES

Greek Easter Cookies

3 1/2 cups ALL-PURPOSE FLOUR, SIFTED

3/4 cup plus 2 tablespoons OLIVE OIL

1 cup ICING SUGAR

1 cup PISTACHIO NUTS, ROUGHLY GROUND

1/3 cup RAISINS, CHOPPED

2 EGGS, LIGHTLY BEATEN

2 tablespoons OUZO OR ORANGE JUICE

2 teaspoons BAKING POWDER

2 teaspoons ANISEED OR CARAWAY SEEDS

2 teaspoons GRATED ORANGE PEEL

pinch SALT

Preheat the oven to 350°F. Beat all the ingredients together in a bowl to form a sticky dough. Knead lightly until smooth and roll into walnut-sized balls. Pat flat and place on a large, greased baking sheet. Bake for 15 to 20 minutes until risen and golden. Cool on a wire rack. Store in an airtight container.

MAKES 36-40 COOKIES

TOP: *Amaretti Biscotti*
BOTTOM: *Greek Easter Cookies*

INDEX

Aïoli
rosemary, with broiled mushrooms 34
with rice and seafood 76
Anchovy(ies)
caramelized onion and radicchio bruschetta 36
with navy beans, oil and lemon 66
Lentil and vegetable broth with anchovy paste 30
paste with broiled tomato and onion pizza 86
Artichoke(s)
prosciutto and goat cheese pizza 86
stuffed 62
Arugula and chicken liver bruschetta 36
Arugula pesto with potato and garlic soup 28
Asparagus, penne, potatoes and tapenade 80
Asparagus and tomato salad, broiled 70
Avocado and smoked chicken salad 70

Baked red bell peppers topped with mozzarella
Bean(s)
fennel and borlotti bean bake 62
navy, with oil, lemon and anchovies 66
and seafood salad, Italian 74
Beef carpaccio 40
Beef with raisins and nuts 58
Bitter salad with Caesar dressing 72
Blinis, smoked salmon, with chive oil 34
Bread
herb and cheese 90
rosemary focaccia 88
tomato and mozzarella 90
Broccoli with pasta and walnuts 78
Bruschetta 36
anchovy, onion and radicchio 36
chicken liver and arugula 36
Butter bean and sage pâté, warm 38
Butter beans with lamb steaks 54

Cabbage, sausages baked with lentils and 54
Caesar salad dressing with bitter salad 72
Camembert with whole baked garlic 40
Caramelized garlic oil 14
Carpaccio, beef 40
Carrot and ginger cake 92
Charmoula with mussel soup 32
Cheese
and herb bread 90
and pesto pizza 84
see also Camembert; goat cheese; Mozzarella
Chicken
with preserved lemon and eggplants 50
smoked chicken and avocado salad 70
tagine with figs, olives and nuts 52
Chicken liver and arugula bruschetta 36
Chick-peas, spinach, raisins and pine nuts 64
Chilled Catalan gazpacho 30
Chili
with homemade tagliatelle 78
shrimp with fennel sauce 48
wicked chili oil 16
Chive oil with smoked salmon blinis 34

Chorizo and radicchio risotto 82
Citrus oil dressing 13
Citrus oils 16
Corn relish with salmon seviche 46
Couscous, fish 42
Crab cakes, New England 44

East-West dressing with marinated scallops 72
Eggplant(s)
dip 38
with chicken and preserved lemon 50
Imam Bayildi 64

Fennel and Borlotti bean bake 62
Fennel sauce 48
Fish 42-8
couscous 42
soupe de poisson 26
Focaccia, rosemary 88
Fritto misto with lemon and thyme mayonnaise 60

Garlic
with homemade tagliatelle 78
and potato soup with arugula pesto 28
whole baked, with Camembert 40
Garlic oil, caramelized 14
Garlic oil, raw 14
Gazpacho, chilled Catalan 30
Goat cheese
artichoke and prosciutto pizza 86
marinated goat cheese salad 68
Greek Easter cookies 92

Harissa paste 22
Herb and cheese bread 90
Herb oil 16

Imam bayildi 64
Italian bean and seafood salad 74

Jambalaya 82

Lamb
souvlaki 52
steaks with butter beans 54
Lemon,
preserved with chicken and eggplants 50
and thyme mayonnaise 60
Lentil and vegetable broth 30
Lentils with sausages and cabbage 54

Marinated goat cheese salad 68
Marinated pork with potatoes 58
Marinated scallops with East-West dressing 72
Mayonnaise 18
lemon and thyme 60
Mozzarella
baked red bell peppers topped with 66
and tomato bread 90
Mullet nicoise, baked 44
Mushrooms
broiled field, with rosemary aïoli 34
oyster, with spaghetti and scallops 80
Mussel soup with charmoula 32

Navy beans with oil, lemon and anchovies 66
New England crab cakes 44

Olea Europea 8
Oleaster olive tree 8
Olio santo 16
Olive oil 9-12
choosing and cooking 11-12
nutrition 10
production 9-10
types of 10-11
virgin and extra-virgin 12
Olive trees 8-9
Olives
with chicken tagine 52
fragrant 24
preserved 24
varieties 9
Onion, anchovy and radicchio bruschetta 36
Onion and tomato pizza, broiled 86
Oriental salad dressing 13

Pasta with broccoli and walnuts 78
Penne with new potatoes, asparagus and tapenade 80
Peppers, baked red bell, topped with mozzarella 66
Pesto 20
and cheese pizza 84
arugula, with potato and garlic soup 28
parsley 20
red 20
Pizza
artichoke, prosciutto and goat cheese 86
basic pizza base 84
broiled tomato and onion, with anchovy paste 86
pesto and cheese 84
Pork, marinated, with potatoes 58
Pork, stuffed tenderloin 56
Potato(es)
and garlic soup with arugula pesto 28
with marinated pork 58
mashed, with thyme oil 66
new, with penne, asparagus and tapenade 80
Prosciutto, artichoke and goat cheese pizza 86

Radicchio, anchovy and onion bruschetta 36
Radicchio and chorizo risotto 82
Rice, with seafood and aïoli 76
Risotto, chorizo and radicchio 82
Roasted tomato soup with cilantro 28
Rosemary aïoli with broiled mushrooms 34
Rosemary focaccia 88

Salad dressing 12-13
Caesar 72
citrus oil 13
creamy 14
East-West 72
Oriental 13
Vinaigrette 13
Salads 68-75
bitter, with Caesar dressing 72

broiled tomato and asparagus 70
broiled vegetable, with skordalià 74
Italian bean and seafood 74
marinated goat cheese 68
seeded yam 70
smoked chicken and avocado 70
Salmon seviche with corn relish 46
Sativa olive tree 8
Sausages, baked with cabbage and lentils 54
Scallops, marinated, and East-West dressing 72
Scallops, spaghetti and oyster mushrooms 80
Sea bream, baked in paper, whole 44
Seafood
Italian bean and seafood salad 74
kebabs, mixed, 48
with rice and aïoli 76
Seeded yam salad 70
Shrimp, chili, with fennel sauce 48
Skordalià 18, 52
with broiled vegetable salad 74
Smoked chicken and avocado salad 70
Smoked salmon blinis with chive oil 34
Soupe de poisson 26
Soups 26-33
chilled Catalan gazpacho 30
lentil and vegetable broth with anchovy paste 30
mussel, with charmoula 32
potato and garlic, with arugula pesto 28
roasted tomato, with cilantro 28
Turkish-style oven 32
Souvlaki 52
Spaghetti, scallops and oyster mushrooms 80
Spinach, chick-peas, raisins and pine nuts 64
Stuffed pork tenderloin 56

Tagliatelle, garlic and chili, homemade 78
Tapenade 22
with penne, new potatoes and asparagus 80
Thyme oil with mashed potato 66
Tomato(es)
and asparagus salad, broiled 70
broiled tomato and onion pizza 86
dried and preserved cherry 24
and mozzarella bread 90
roasted tomato soup with cilantro 28
Turkish-style oven soup 32

Vegetable dishes 60-7
Vegetable salad with skordalià, broiled 74
Vinaigrette 13

Walnut and olive oil cake 92
Walnut paste 22
with pasta and broccoli 78
Whole sea bream baked in paper 44
Wicked chili oil 16

Yam, seeded salad 70